The Love Language of Plants

To all the things that grow.

I am forever grateful for your guidance.

The Love Language of Plants

Stories of Becoming

Written by a Human and Her Plants

Sydney Kale

Foreword by Peter Webb

Contents

A Note on Names, Pronouns, and Capitalization

If you've decided to arrive at this section before reading, you're welcome to continue. However, I also invite you to read the rest of the book first so you have the opportunity to experience how the naming, gendering, and capitalization practices make you feel before I tell you what they mean to me. But what I share here may feel like a desired container to guide you through your reading.

The names presented for each plant were chosen by myself and the plant. As an expression of our relationship, non-Latin names feel the most familiar and comforting, and may be recognizable to you. When you meet a plant, feel welcome to ask what they want to be called.

I use gendered pronouns (they/them, she/her, he/him) to refer to plants instead of as "it." To usher the plants into this coveted section of our lexicon is to acknowledge more-than-human agency and personhood. The same is done on behalf of capitalization of names, to share them the honor bestowed upon a proper noun. I am calling them by their name, not their label. I am calling them by who they are and what they are made of.

Notably, throughout the book and my experiences with plants, pronouns might suddenly change or flow. This is not because the plant suddenly changed gender; male/female is not synonymous with masculine/feminine. It is because our relationship changed, or the way our energies resonated with each other changed. The choice of pronouns is a representation of my own processing and honoring of how we relate to each other and express ourselves and each other as individuals through a very human mode of articulation. I can't say that a plant cares about pronouns and capitalization. But I explore this practice as a ritualistic expression of honor from my culture to theirs.

For more information on languaging our relationships with those we share Earth with, I would suggest reading Robin Wall Kimmerer's "Learning the Grammar of Animacy." Robin alternatively offers pronouns ki/kin to "signify a being of living Earth." The practice she offers is simple and beautiful, but I have not yet adopted it into my own grammar practice as it doesn't fully represent my experiences and sentiments. What doesn't feel authentic to me may feel authentic to you. What feels authentic may also change and shift over time. It's okay to be curious and explore where possibilities and richness of experience are taking you.

Foreword

In and through this beautiful collection of essays, Sydney shares the intimate space of relationships she has experienced with plants. These are not just stories but sensitive tales of a shared intimate reality of being; tales of encounters beyond the human realm.

Plants and animals are our elders. They have been living on planet Earth for much longer than we who are still a young species. It is no fanciful idea that maybe they have a wisdom in which we can share. Somehow, we have come to assume that they are just decoration or at best our food. Throughout history, many have told different stories about their experiences with them, but in this book, the encounters are more than stories; they are shared experiences offered in such a way that we can feel them for ourselves, each in our own manner; something like the profound experience of myth. How can words relate life other than inciting it?

Most authors seek to awaken in some way a resonance within others or at least the mind of their readers. In and through her encounters with plants, Sydney has artfully shaped an experiential space into which we are invited. A space between the words themselves where we can savor something very special. These conversations are alive, and no doubt each reader will find themself resonating with the plants rather than rationalising them. These are relationships to be experienced; sort of like tasting complexity, or catching a perfume that defies the description of passion.

Plants are ancient beings. Their languages are so different from our own, and yet we are intricately interwoven together. We breathe them and ingest them, while imitating them unknowingly in all we call science, architecture, and medicine. Through our philosophies and religions, we attempt to define our way in space and time, which is in fact a daily activity of plants. They have no need for a brain as they live interdependently; their orientation is one of sharing, much more than of competition. Their philosophy is of life and death; it is so intrinsic that these ancient, resilient beings are here in the 21st century,and will probably be here, quietly doing what they do, for millennia after we have gone.

We could humbly say that they know a thing or two, which may indeed help us in our reflections and actions. (No wonder many kneel as they do in their gardens). We know that this is true, but forget the simplicity of their strategies. They are interdependent individuals in impermanent communities where they only grasp with their roots.

As a foreword to these beautifully related encounters which Sydney shares, I bring an invitation to breathe into the spaces between the words she has carefully chosen, as their flavor is where we can most deeply experience our own understanding of their messages. Experiences of timeless space, wisdom and pleasures which can defy any description.

You must have this experience.

Peter Webb

Prologue

The idea for this book was conceived a little less than two years before we started writing it. The idea was gifted to me by the plants themselves, at the beginning of a journey into human and plant relationship. I told the plants that I wanted to get to know them, and they told me where to start. But there were other things I had to learn first, before these words would come to be. I had to go on journeys through deserts and rainforests and mountains and beaches. I had to travel through pages and pages of books; through lectures; through personal conversations whose privacy was shadowed by the universe listening in.

I ate plants. I drank plants. I sat with plants. I gardened and tended. I watched plants make their first peek into the spring sun and I watched them die. I sang to them and learned their songs. I asked them questions and shared pieces of myself in return. I danced and walked and ran. I laughed, I cried, and I imagined. We paid close attention to each other, and to ourselves. We spoke unfamiliar words and tried new kinds of hugs. All of the new and unfamiliar eventually transformed into a deep familiarity, as if this was the way it always has been, and was always supposed to be.

What is the love language of plants? This was my research question. I was in my second master's program studying Movement, Mind, and Ecology at Schumacher College, a small ecological school in England. I was living in Texas at the time, completing my coursework online. When I started the program, I was a disgruntled activist who just completed a year of fundraising, petitioning, and lobbying. And while I wanted to make change, to protect the places that I cared about and everything in them, I felt like there was something human missing in the kind of numbers game my political activist organization was asking me to play. So, I went searching for it – the human and the mystical – in my small studio apartment in Austin, Texas.

The plants and I learned and searched for meaning together. I didn't notice them at first, but eventually their voices became deafening. I didn't know exactly where we were going, but I was along for the ride.

In my first semester of my fourth return to formal education I wrote an essay about Kudzu and feral ecologies. I learned that, like plants labeled as invasive, we, too, become problematic when we are removed from our element. We've forgotten where home is, and what home is supposed to feel like. We've forgotten who we are and who we're supposed to be. At least some of us have.

I was learning that maybe something human was missing not because it wasn't there but because we've been denying our own humanness. We're running away from it, retreating into our homes in a way we didn't used to.

In *A Honeybee Heart Has Five Openings*, author Helen Jukes reflects on the origins of the word home, writing, "Home referred not to a building or even a geographical location, but a state of being; a place at the heart of real...A place from which worlds could be founded; a place where meanings are made."

Even those who recognize that we are a part of nature and not something separate from it sometimes believe that the Earth is better off when we leave no trace. That our humanness spoils nature. That 'everything is as it should be', except what is human. We hold these beliefs, often unconsciously, and fail to notice all the ways that the world tries to touch us back and leave its trace on our humanness.

I learned about the erasure of Indigenous stewardship on the land we call North America. Never having seen a land in such a lush and manicured state, the colonizers didn't think to attribute human activity to its flourishing. I learned that John Muir, the Father of Our National Park System, in the words of Lyla June, "repeatedly characterizes Indigenous People as a blemish on the face of a 'pristine nature.'" So parks were set aside as pure wilderness, with humanness removed, instilling the idea that nature is better off when we are not a part of it.

But I feel like I am a part of it. I have seen what human hands can do when they reach deep in the soil. I heard stories about the beauty that can be left behind where a human treads. I have listened to the plants tell stories of being alive and reaching out to those who will listen.

I wanted to partake in the diplomacy of plants and the politics of nature. I wanted to know what it really felt like to be human. The plants reminded me what sunshine feels like against my skin. They reminded me what it feels like to be gently pelted by the clouds' tears. They reminded me what it feels like to be brushed by an animal and hear the humming of a foraging bee. They are qualified to remind me because they know.

As a tired activist who was trying to re-learn who I was, I started to seek counsel in the nonhuman. I found myself drawn to what was supposed to be nothing like me. Plants seem so still and quiet. They cover the Earth with their presence, but do not impose themselves unduly; they do not mis-manage and over-extract from the land, as humans have increasingly done.

And yet plants *do* participate in life. They do not impose but offer their voice in conversation with the world. Their language is colorful. Their language is fragrant. Their language is loud, but you have to be so quiet to hear it.

By quiet, I don't mean invisible, turned off, vacant, or still. A plant's voice arrives in a thundering gentleness that you feel for in the darkness. To be quiet is to be turned on, tuned in, susceptible, ajar. And they participate in life, intimately and visibly. Plants are stewards of the Earth and those around them. Plants take care of us.

Taking care is not their sole purpose, however. They do not exist *for* us, but *with* us. A plant's life is valuable and meaningful because they are alive, and because they exist as they are in the communities they are in. Craig Holdrege says, "[A plant] is always showing you itself and the world out of which it is grown. That world has become part of it, and without it it could not be."

Plants hold a beautiful power to become who they are in the place that they are. Philosopher Michael Marder says that plants "materially articulate the Earth and the Sky and express the beings around them." They bloom and emerge and unfold in such a way that is delicately timed and intimately attuned to place and all that place contains. They know how to be in the place that they're in; to be native to place.

I have not always been so good at being in the place that I'm in. But the plants have been teaching me what it feels like to be rooted — in place, and also in self. They have taken me on a journey of learning to embody authenticity and be a part of the story I'm telling.

Plants have always been a part of the story. They've been here for millions of years. They found land and became one with it. They found insects and became one with them. They found humans and watched and observed. They held our hands, clothed our children, healed our wounds. They sheltered us from the stormy rains and tickled our feet at sunrise. And when life showed up at their doorstep, they welcomed its passage through.

Plants emerge out of darkness, find their bearings, and chase life with those around them. And they call. They call to their neighbors, and to the birds and the moths and the bees. They call to their loved ones and tell stories of great triumph and tranquil defeat. They cry when one of their own goes back to the Earth. And they rejoice as the Sun rises in the morning as they do when the stars come out to watch over them.

In my time as a student of the human education system and the plants, I've found a beautiful world in the weavings of plant teachings and scientific ones. I've also learned that we can explore our world in such a way that allows plants to tell their own stories.

Plant voices come in many forms. I learned that plants craft their means of communication before sending their words out into the place they're in. By combining small chemical units to create chemical compounds, plants release these compounds of intricate and intentional meaning out into the soil and into the air. As they evolve, and their place evolves, they assign new meaning to existing chemical compounds to represent novel contexts and experiences. As they evolve, so, too, does their language.

They also have population-specific dialects. Sagebrush, an aromatic shrub that grows in the deserts and mountainsides of western North America, has demonstrated this phenomenon, having been observed sending messages to their neighbors to arm their defenses when under the attack of herbivores. The authors of a 2021 study suggest that their findings "seem to indicate [that varying] chemotypes can be considered examples of language differences based on relatedness, suggesting that language is shaped by the context in which it is used and in which it develops." Plants represent their home; they express the place they are in. And in doing so, they express the way they relate to each other, and all that that place presents to them.

One of the things a place presents to plants is death. To be alive is, ultimately, to die. The plants know better than anyone that participation in life is intimately linked with death. One of the love languages of a plant is certainly death, though not in quite the same way that death is the particular love language of mushrooms, whose function is to break down and reintegrate dead matter.

The plants say, *If you want to understand death, you need to know how to live in this body of yours that spans well beyond your skin.*

They say, *Learn who you are. You are ecosystems; you are multitudes. You are rocks and rivers and Aspens and Marigolds. You are rain and laughter and Owls and mountains. If you know what the universe feels like, you'll never lose your bearings. If you know what life feels like, you'll never lose your bearings.*

Plants offer a gentle hand in our attempts to live and a soft bed when our time comes to rest. They know what it means to die, and it's a teaching they are willing to share. They are well acquainted with death.

Flowers like those of the Pawpaw, a little known yet culturally significant fruit tree native to the eastern United States, have tuned into death for survival. To attract their pollinators - carrion flies - they release chemical compounds containing putrecine and cadaverine to mimic the smells of decomposition that draw them in. They have come to know death through smelling it, and through evolving with it.

Scientist Rupert Sheldrake writes that "dying cells play a major part in the regulation of plant growth, releasing the plant hormone auxin as they break down in the process of 'programmed cell death'. Inside growing plants, new wood cells dissolve themselves as they die, leaving their cellulose walls as microscopic tubes through which water is conducted in stems, roots and veins of leaves. I discovered that auxin is produced as cells die, that dying cells stimulate more growth; more growth leads to more death, and hence to more growth."

Death makes space for life. Perhaps death also holds life in a gentle brutality that beckons a kind of letting go — a letting go that humans often struggle to grasp. We can talk about the big birth and the big death. But plants tell stories about the little deaths we die every day, that make space for our unfolding into ourselves and the world, infinitely.

I learned that plants listen to the water that they drink. Their roots know what water sounds like, and they move toward the sound even before they come to touch it.

Just as roots can hear the song of water, flowers listen to the songs sung by the flapping wings of their pollinators. In a 2019 experiment with Evening Primrose, flowers that heard recordings of the flapping wings of

Honeybees produced nectar with a higher sugar content than those grown in silence. Flowers can sense the ones that they feed.

They know what their flying friends sound like, even before they touch one another. A grounded, negatively charged flower feels the positive charge of flying pollinators. The static energy created by the opposing charges sends pollen flying to stick to the hairs of the ones who draw near. As their pollinators approach, a flower will increase the power of their charge, lifting their voice. They also release perfumes; some pungent and sugary, some gentle and aromatic, some smelling sweetly of death. The pollinators know these smells, and greet the calls of their friends.

When the flower and the flying pollinator do touch, the flower changes her song and alters her electrical charge for several moments following their meeting. Pollinators can read these charges and, upon approach, will favor the songs of those flowers who have not yet been met. These are the flowers who are still full of pollen and nectar.

Plants also know who is around them. When their roots encounter those of another plant, they can identify whether it is kin (one of their own offspring); a friendly but non-related plant; or an enemy. Small plants have millions of root tips while a tree can have hundreds of billions. A plant's root system is, in many ways, similar to a human's nervous system. Touching the Earth, roots allow plants to understand their home through tactile cognition. They listen to the world deep underground.

They listen to the sound of water and share whispers with their mycelial companions in the soil.

Sometimes, I wonder what it is like to sit as a plant does and feel their entire world. Sometimes, I close my eyes and feel myself root into the ground and stretch toward the sky. What I find is not immobility, but patience and intention. These can be realised passively and actively - both approaches being valid, and sacred.

I was taught the Northern European Mystery Tradition of Utiseta, which translates to "sitting out" or "sitting on the land." Traditionally, one would sit in a sacred, secluded place in nature overnight and connect with the wisdom and spirits of the land. This kind of knowing is precious. It's in these moments that I feel closer to sitting in the way a plant does, knowing the Earth and the Sky as they do.

It is through a nameless knowing and a humble understanding of place that the plants help create the sky. They have lungs called stomata, on average 300 of them per square millimeter of leaf, through which they exchange their breath with the world. They take the carbon dioxide which we exhale, and transform it into the precious oxygen that fills our lungs and our atmosphere with the potential for life. That precious oxygen is full of the plants themselves and the aromatic messages they send.

Martin Burd says that we have "the great privilege of eavesdropping on the colorful and fragrant conversations between the flowers and the birds and the insects."

What a privilege it is to eavesdrop, and learn the language of plants.

"The love language of plants," said the plants. *"That's where you have to begin."*

Love's purpose lies only in itself. Love flows through everything. The flow is not what creates the meaning of love; rather, it is through the meaning deeply embedded in the fabric of the universe that love finds its expression. Love, perhaps, is you and me; in our element, in our home.

Maybe love is different than I had always imagined it to be. The Neo-Confusian philosopher Zhu Xi says that "throughout the universe there is no qi without li, nor li without qi." Qi is the flow of energy and matter. Li, which originally referred to the "swirling patterns visible in a piece of jade," are "the principles by which the qi is organized." Could love be li?

Erotic ecologist Andreas Weber says that "love is not a feeling, but the characteristic of a productive relationship." That "ecosystems are love stories. Our most profound ways to relate and to feel, to exchange and to be touched, are ecological forms of gifting life, of loving." That "love is a practice that makes others alive and, through this, enlivens yourself."

I didn't know any of this about love when the plants first told me about the idea for this book. *"The love language of plants,"* they said. *"That's where you have to begin."* But how?

Do plants love? What does such love look like? What does it feel like? What is love? I had more questions than I had answers, and no idea where to begin. This was a space in which I had yet to find my bearings. It felt unfamiliar. It felt dark and quiet. But it is often in the dark and quiet that we find the most vibrant wisdom. It can't be lured, it can't be called. You wait and watch as elements of this space begin to make themselves known to you, like lightning bugs orchestrating gentle vision in the night.

Even in my search for the love language of plants, I denied myself the beauty of humanness. I was sure that the plant love I was looking for would be unfamiliar; it would be a love that was not human, and therefore pure and right and just. I was still pessimistic about humanity. This love wouldn't be human because humanness didn't feel very beautiful. It didn't look very beautiful either. But aren't we allowed to be beautiful? Aren't we supposed to be?

I didn't want to find manifestations of human behaviors of love; I wanted to find plant love. How do you find something when you don't know what you're looking for? They must know something about their experience of love and be able to share. And thankfully, they were willing.

The plants said, *"If you want to know the love language of plants, then fall in love with a plant."*

In falling in love with a plant, I was forced to reckon with my humanness. The words on this page emerged through co-becoming — a co-becoming of human and plant as individuals, and in relationship. Co-becoming is not simply a methodology. It is a way of living that acknowledges life's relationality and allows me to emerge as a product of the many relationships I do not exist without. It is living as the embodiment of kinship and entanglement. It is the acknowledgement that in every moment, I am becoming and unfolding and, like a plant, my becoming and unfolding is delicately attuned to place and everything in it. Our emergence is relational.

I wanted to represent plants on their own terms, in their own plantness. But this could not happen without my representing plants in the way I have come to know them.

As an academic and a writer, I practice co-authorship with plants. What we create together is woven in collaboration with two lives; two ways of knowing; two ways of expressing life. It is a work of art that is not entirely human but not entirely plant. We experience each other through each other, and then put words on a page in an attempt to represent such moments - moments that words can imagine yet never actually realize. Andreas Weber says, "Nature is not a place that shields us from feeling; rather, it is a refuge where we can experience our true emotions. Plants and animals help us discover significant things about ourself. In them, we find our own inwardness."

The plants and I talked. And we listened. Our bodies and our imaginations lit up as we observed each other, embraced each other, and listened to each other's voices. When you encounter a plant's soul, you have the opportunity to feel their spirit and listen to their voice. But you also have the opportunity to encounter your own soul, to feel the quality of your thoughts, the flowing mosaic of somatic experience blinking and settling throughout your body. In observing the aliveness of a plant, I encounter my own.

The plants offer a different kind of relationship and a different kind of friendship.

I wrote my master's dissertation with Damiana about the love language of plants. We explored what it looks like for a human and a plant to go on such a journey together, and what the implications are for science and academia in asking such questions. In this first work of writing I ever shared with the plants, we wrote: *"Maybe this is the love language of plants. They not only love through teaching, but they love through friendship. I do not know if this is the full answer, but it is not the answer I was expecting to receive. I have been so hell-bent on finding this love that is so alien and foreign to me, maybe because I wanted it to be as alien and foreign as plants seem. If they are so different, so must be their love. And yes it may be different, but if love really is a force intrinsic to life, it would be accessible to all beings in all forms. If I can learn the language of the flowers and the trees and the rocks and the rivers, then I can learn the languages of love."*

It makes sense that Damiana came forward to write this dissertation with me. She's a heart-opener and an aphrodisiac. I experienced this energy, but it manifested in a different way than I would have assumed. She taught me how to trust myself and my intuition. She showed me what it feels like to be in my body, in my home. She sensitized me to the touches of the world. She showed me what a plant's love felt like.

Plant love feels like a cool, welcome breeze on a hot, balmy day. Plant love feels like locking eyes with someone you know, and feeling safe enough to blush. Plant love feels simple—blameless, humble, sheer. Satish Kumar says that to live elegantly and simply is to spend more time dancing, creating poetry, and imagining.

I fell in love with plants. I also fell in love with myself. I've joked before that my academic work is healing me. That the plants knew the only way to get me to do this work was to tell me I had to get a doctorate degree. It doesn't feel as much like a joke anymore.

What a thing it is to love and be loved. The word love has been used to describe pleasure, admiration, and trust. It holds a collection of feelings and experiences, some I'm familiar with and some I may never encounter. We say that sometimes love hurts, too. But it's not the love that hurts, it's the fear of losing it. It's the pain we feel when we rip off a piece of ourselves to give to another, and we forget to call it back home when it's time is done. But it's okay, the little pieces of love out there make home where they land when they aren't called back. They find themselves a warm cocoon of Earth and let time heal the wound from where they'll burst forth.

Plants teach through unconventional means. I had to learn what it felt like to be in my body again, as the touch of plants infiltrated my feelings and emotions and dreams and thoughts. The plants took me to places that feel like when a dream comes to life. They spoke languages I didn't know existed. Some of them had words; some of them didn't. Some of them I understood; some of them I didn't.

We sat together. We danced together. We dreamed together. I sat at their feet, as a student. I saw myself as a small child. I saw myself as I am now. They showed me parts of their world, and in doing so, I encountered my own world. My teacher, Jean Schneider, says we should open the door when the plants knock. And keep opening the door. And keep knocking. The plants know when we are open to listening, and they start speaking to us.

The plants have a story to tell. It has been a privilege to listen to and a privilege to share. They become and unfold over a lifetime. And in doing so, they transform into something that is irreplaceable to life; something that is beautiful and small and unimaginably large. They transform into something ancient and present. They find home. And they know it. And they live it.

The meandering journey through plant love and plant voice brought us to the words on these pages. If you listen, you can hear their voice as you read.

Words are a funny human medium to try to fit plant being and plant relationship into. Words have meaning, but that meaning is always somewhat fluid and ambiguous, shifting its shape according to the context and interpretations of its readers. There are a million ways to understand the universe, and you are one of them. And so are the plants. And the bees. And the worms. And the ants. And the groundhogs. And the toad. David Abram defines 'making sense' as "to enliven the senses and [renew] and [rejuvenate] one's felt awareness of the world."

While some may cry anthropomorphism, I wonder why we deny rather than rejoice the moment that shared experiences are realized between the human and the more-than-human. Would it threaten our sense of humanness —or, conversely, support it — to know that a plant can also know, remember, think, love? The words on these pages do 'personify' plants. But a person, after all, as defined by John Locke, is "a thinking intelligent Being, that has reason and reflection, and can consider itself as itself, the same thinking thing in different times and places."

Maybe to personify a plant means to see them for who they are: animate, intelligent, feeling, and thinking. Maybe it's not only short-sighted but ultimately wrong of us to believe that we're in a position to determine the extent of another being's subjectivity, or the quality of their experience. Michael Hall offers instead that "the language of sentience can be viewed, not as a self projection, but…as a *bridge* between two *types* of being…This language is a form of empathy, employed in the service of building relationships of care and kinship. In essence it provides the *sameness* required for flourishing relationships in the face of obvious morphological difference."

In *The Flowering Wand*, Sophie Strand shares her belief in an animism of chaotic difference: "It is an understanding that my being alive does not mean I should assume that the aliveness of the hill or the river or the wild roses is the same flavor as my aliveness. Knowing that a stone is alive keeps me alive. And knowing that a stone is alive differently than me keeps me asking questions, keeps me humble and curious and open to surprise."

I believe that there are different flavors of aliveness inside of us that we have yet to taste. A plant and only a plant knows what it is to be a plant. I can imagine, and they can offer me glimpses into their world. But the plants don't want me to be a plant. They don't need me to be a plant. They need me to be human.

It doesn't feel like such a crazy thing anymore: to love someone as they are for who they are. Plants demonstrate greatness for us when it aligns with our definitions of demonstrated greatness, like intentionality, creativity, and mathematics. But they don't have to. There is greatness in aliveness, and there is greatness in being. Those are demonstrations that you don't have to look for, because they are happening all around us.

A plant's voice doesn't start and end with you. Let the plants be plants and let humans be humans. There are stories out there, hidden deep within the universe or hiding in plain sight. I hope you take this book as an invitation to start listening.

Damiana

If you want to know love, lay across my body and feel your edges melt away until the illusion of one ending so another can begin fades away. Feel a soft pillow rise up to meet your weight. Let me use your heart as kindling to ignite a fire whose embers will never die, even when the flames subside.

If you want to know love, breathe in an earthy sweetness that is only found wafting from my tender tissue. Let it kiss you on the cheek and dissolve, not before lingering in your nostrils like a bee finding rest in the warm cocoon of a flower it cannot help but understand.

If you want to know love, look for eros. To find it, travel past the grove of Pines 50 miles long, over the ridgeline that communes with the Clouds, to the right of the Red-Headed Woodpecker that serenades and calls the forest in quick knocks, and then look under the dampest, grayest rock where you'll find a Worm writhing in the cool wet of the Earth.

The spectrum of experience we have waiting to entangle us is not as limited as we once believed. Experience fully. Experience uninhibited. Experience because you have nothing else to do.

If you want to know love, dance like nobody is watching. Move your body until you can't move it anymore, and do it for someone. Anyone. Let it be ugly. Let it be beautiful. A dedication in the form of a writhing prophecy that will only always come true.

If you want to know love, let it torture you. Look for it, even when you know you won't find it, even if just to catch a glimpse. Join me in unknowing. I will entertain your deepest questions, and I will help you look for the answer, delighting in the secret, knowing of its inexistence. There are a million ways to tell someone that snow is white. There are a million ways to tell someone you love them. All of them are right.

Damiana. Damiana. Damiana, Damiana, Damiana.

A persistent chorus that does not cease, even after concession. Just as love is an inescapable, unrelenting force, so too is the one that wants to share it with you.

So, you want to know the love language of plants? All you have to do is ask.

Take rest in joy. Find shelter in the morning birdsong. Offer life at the day's horizon, and offer your consciousness as honey, warmed and dripping, at the day's end.

Something sweet lives inside you. It seeps out of your pores. It is stolen by a glance, spilling out between you and the world in front of you. It hardens behind an unfinished sentence that discovers all care as it slips into all that there is.

When you find it, hold it close to your chest. The sweetness inside of you is alive. It moves and breathes; it must be cared for and loved and respected. It enjoys sitting and cradling a warm cup of tea as you confess your latest hopes and dreams. It finds tranquility in a languid, seemingly endless bath where you let the warmth seep in rather than attempt to pick up the pieces. It smiles on as it watches you realize the thing you're looking at is a treasure you desperately want to clasp.

The sweetness inside of you is alive.

Thistle

In a clearing sits a friend, solemn and regal; patient; waiting. Her roots are digging deep into the earth; her stem is reaching out and up to the sky that nourishes her. When Thistle wraps you in her warm embrace, she shows you where your soft spots lie and where your thorns bite back, hiding scars, a sign of something to be protected that once was not.

Her roots sink into my skull, inoculating my thoughts with images of dancing in fields, catching the wind, and purple.

Her roots can release the most compacted of souls. And yet, she teaches me how to catch the wind, a master at occupying the spaces between the fleeting and the settled. The procedure of such an inoculation releases pressure that has been lying in wait, undetected but brooding and present. Roots take in, but they also release.

Something so gentle can also be tough. Clarity, assurance, and assertion of self do not necessitate severity. Knowing oneself makes it easier to be known by others. Gentleness does not imply availability for the taking.

In this world, the past loops back to meet the present, making haste to join the endless possibility of the future.

Thistle is a holder and creator of space. She carries the instructions for how to make space for oneself; an invaluable lesson for those who tend to prioritize making space for others. Thistle is covered in spines and is willing to offer a spine to those without. Thistle holds her own. The space she has created can be observed by all but entered by only some. How do you hold space for trauma and simultaneously release it?

Sitting quietly on a forest floor or in a grassy field, Thistle holds space for the symphony of life around, turning the sweet nectar of sunshine and cool drip of rain into sensuous and resuscitated matter, tranquility on display and preciously protected, a laborer at peace with life's work.

Thank you, Thistle, for introducing me to your space and helping me find my own. You have enlivened my days with the joy of myself and knowing there is someone there, whether or not I have the energy to give and whether or not I have the maturity to meet you.

I am Sydney Kale, friend of Thistle.

I am Thistle, friend of Earth, tender of disturbed soils and souls, and conduit of space and truth. Hear my name over and over and over and over.

And after all is done, no words hang in the air, only space,

    growing,

        morphing,

            expanding

                and contracting,

                holding and letting go.

Some memories cannot be anything but

held; others are crafted without the

binding that fastens them to your soul.

This is not a failure in design.

Sydney Kale

Passionflower

When I greet plants in magical places, I am always tiny, smaller than the insects scurrying across the ground and cascading through the air. I am small; I climb up the plant to sit in its flower, or swim in a pool created within a mushroom on the face of a tree trunk.

Today, I sat with Thistle, waiting to be introduced to a new friend. The introduction was warm; two old friends and one new one huddled together in a warm embrace, waiting for the human one to transplant herself onto the petals of another.

Seated atop Passionflower, I was surrounded by columns millions of years in the making, lifting the forest from its floor into canopies of unimaginable heights. Passionflower slowly marched through the forest, willfully and intently. Each step beats slow and low like a shamanic drum. There was a low humming in the foreground. As we walked, I looked up into the trees, too tall to even see their canopy from my vantage point. They stood patiently waiting, for what I may never know; a presence silently imbuing a homecoming.

Passionflower's smell is hard to resist. She carries with her a deep sweetness of a caramelization held within a delicate, tendrilled frame. This deep sweetness is of the kind that knows what it means to be.

"Where are we going?" I asked.

"To the place of light."

"What's in the place of light?"

"Flowers."

An opening in the grand cathedral of trees created a doorway of light, and the light spilled out in its abundance. Within the warm sun danced thousands of flowers and bees, a ballroom of slow-dancing lovers, slipping partner to partner to share their lush offerings. The bees were curious of my presence but did little more than observe and depart, not falling out of line in a dance that could only be choreographed by desire and a conversation deeply embedded in the artistry of nature's hues.

"Tell us something about yourself."

Lost for words in a place that had none, I spoke, "I am a flower, too. I bloom, and I die over and over and over again."

"We are of the same blood," the regal flower I sat atop confirmed my musings.

Lost in a vision of color and light, my body awakened with the low buzz of my new friend's tantalizing electricity.

More. I was given more.

More. I was given more.

Even more.

My skin had erupted in the buzzing of a soft, static energy akin to humming cotton balls. My ears rang deeper than my skull. The boundary of my skin against boundaryless space began to dissolve. When we finally pulled away from each other, my heart skipped a beat, settling into the solitude of my own scaffolding and the excitement of a new acquaintance.

Sequoia

Trees are timeless. Or at least they appear so to humans because our lives are so much quicker and shorter than theirs. Their bodies encapsulate vast swaths of time. They hold the slumbering memory of a life unfolded from a seed, cradling within it an untamed memory. The rings of its trunk are a treasury of information. Their deep-reaching roots entomb the past; a record of desires, encounters, choices, interactions - all captured in very instant.

The body of a tree is a shrine to its own life, and a map of the passage of time around it.

I am the Earth's clockmaker. I do not keep time. Time cannot be kept, nor wants to be. Instead, I document time, and in each annotation, a million moments dwell in one infinite present.

Documentation is the destruction and creation of the infinite present.

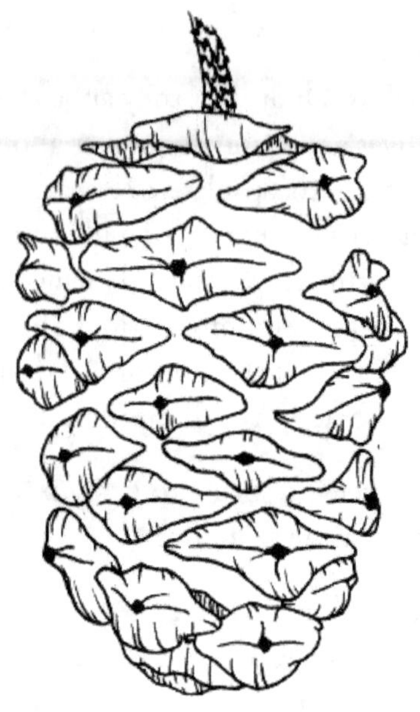

A tree holds a million pasts in one infinite, fossilized present.

You might already know this, but plants came long before humans did. Humans are the children of the earth. Plants are the elders. They carry a deep and ancient wisdom within each living cell. Plants can only tell the stories they know, and we can only hear the ones we don't. Encoded in life is the feeling of experience, tirelessly vacillating between moments of awareness and moments of surrender.

Making sense is a means, not an end. The process of making sense itself becomes the object, obscuring the thing as such. Making sense is a beautiful and profound journey, but don't forget to depart from making sense into a blissful innocence of unknowing what you know.

In a place of no knowledge, you stumble across understanding.

In a place of no knowledge, knowledge is still there. But in this place, it cannot be captured. Knowledge floats, only to be seen, only to be understood.

In this place, you see things for what they are, not for how you try to make them. I told you, there is meaning all around us. In glimpses and glimmers, meaning makes itself known. It cannot be made known by anything other than itself.

In this place, what is known trembles in each cell. The deep rumble of primordial sound. When you take a moment to listen, you'll find a formula for life so simple and so elegant that it cannot be held. It slips through your fingers, and you watch as it slowly and gracefully tumbles through the air. Each time your fingers come close to grasping it, the puff of air produced by your desire sends it pirouetting in the other direction. This dance proceeds until you finally decide to join it in its freefall. I sing to you across this composition, bearing a perception that is not within your repertoire.

I am your elder. And I know how to make myself heard. If you don't hear me, it's because you aren't listening.

I am your elder. And I know how to make myself heard.

Through the ages and sliding behind each word are presences unbeholden. The authors of experience sit at your doorstep, marveling at the possibilities of infinity. This moment right now is a possibility materialized.

We will say it over and over, as many times as we are asked, as long as we are asked. Is it clear yet? Do you understand? Have you noticed the patterns, the dips and curves gliding across the page? Did you hear the same words over and over and over again in languages new and unfamiliar until you finally heard the one word that clung to your understanding, causing each word that came before to stop and slow, drifting into your field of awareness? Do you smell that, the scent of friendship, baked bread, warmth, a crisp river speckled with white fluffy stirring, your ancestors, stillness, the sun, the Earth, Sequoia's breath? Did you feel that? Did you feel life brushing past?

Infinity is not something you're in, but it's what you are.

You, too, can hold The Memoir of All Times. Open the book and smell its pages. That smell is the smell of one infinite lifetime, aging and fermenting, sweetened with the present, wafting toward the future.

Yellow Lotus

One being that holds a million more. A being that demonstrates the permanence of transformation. A pleasure center within the wet entrails of the Earth, found on the edges of bodies, lightly grazing, always on the verge. Each breath swirls downward, gently but intentionally, brushing against the tenderness of body. Each breath tethers you to the world.

Show me what it looks like to bloom as if you are taking your first breath after plunging into icy cold water. Show me what it feels like to bloom infinitely and ceaselessly. Show me what it feels like to breathe into awakening. Show me what it looks like to ground yourself in release. Show me what it feels like to be reincarnated as myself.

"You're torturing yourself with joy and exhilaration," she says. Find calm in the gentle caress of existence. Find calm in what is gentle. With each inhalation of the pheromones of the world, you encounter a soul that can only be known through attention to the moment it lives in. Lotus's scent is gentle, a representation of a purity that is not defined by an absence of contamination. *"Reconsider the definition of purity,"* she says.

Movement lies like a low rumble in the fabric of reality. Let it awaken every molecule you possess so that you may greet life with sincerity and awareness. What we are made of quakes and yawns with a fathomless intensity. What we are made of lies deep in the bones of the universe. As our own little pockets of universe, we reach for what makes us ourselves. We reach for what we believe we were born to be. We reach for what we believe is our self in spite and in praise of oneness. A plant reaches for the Earth and the Sky; for what it is and what it will always be. We are made in the image of life. The plants say, *"I am the sky. I am the soil. I am the creek bed on a balmy spring day. I am a mountain standing guard for freedom on all sides. I am a mountain lion, pawing the darkness of night. I am a sparrow, seeking warmth in the cavities of the Earth."*

Reconsider the definition of purity. Some say Lotus arises from the muck as the antithesis of it. *"No,"* she says, *"I am the muck. I am crafted from the soft wet depths from where my sacred imagination reminded me where I should go. And I took the muck, brought it to the surface, and transformed it into something you can't stop looking at."*

To every drum, there should be a rattle. With each burial is the decomposition of life into infinity. The possibility of becoming never ends. What you are made of will make the universe time after time. The body, you should know, is a portal to infinity. The mind is the vessel that carries you.

Reconsider the definition of purity. I dare you to dance in front of a mirror in a sacred ritual that whispers among the slumbering streets of night and bursts forth from a place of well-being and ugly truths in the warm pool of sunshine. Anoint yourself with oil and cry out your name, whichever one arrives at your lips first.

And then meditate.

Sit in a silent moment of stillness. Close your bloom. Protect what the good day made for you until it is time to forgive and celebrate its liberation. Close your bloom so that you can open it again. Within this slow dance, you find yourself attuned to a cycle lying in wait while we fumble across fabrication. Be in flower

I am human. And to be human is to carry, so be careful what you pick up.

"If you want to write," she said, *"let's write."*

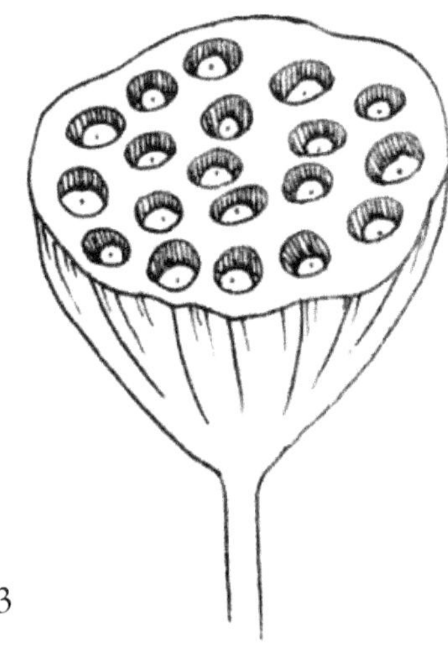

Cedar

Have you ever danced while sitting still?

I remember seeing you across the way. You looked at me like you knew me. You looked at me like we were each other's home. Your existence looked at me and pierced every piece of my tissue until all that was left was a will to live and a curiosity about how to do it. When stripped of my frame, what remains is a life that will, in fact, never stop living.

Every fiber of my being was pulled in a magnetic embrace that was as solid and quivering as the nearby honeysuckle surrendering to the breeze.

Your presence spoke to me in a thousand words that will never be translatable by human tongue, but can only be known by a gaze that escapes the grasp of the eyes. Open them. Close them. It doesn't matter. I assure you will see all the same.

Sitting beneath your boughs, I danced. The colony of grass that blanketed the floor around you danced. They danced by the sunlight bouncing off the gentle dew dipping in the wind and in the joy of communal exaltation of existence. They sang a silent song that rises to climax and reminds you that it's okay not to sing or swell alongside them if you don't want to. The joy of the moment will only meet your present in the absence of pursuit. Joy lives in the present; you will never find it in the future, no matter how hard you try.

You showed me what it was like to dance and be held without ever having to leave my body.

Every one of your pores sang with mine. And when I saw you the next day, I knew you. And you saw me. And together we saw, and we greeted, and we thanked, and we held. Something so fortified can still dance. Something so fortified can still soften by the touch of the world. Something so fortified can know and see without imposing its truth on the rest of the world. Its truth sits in wait for the weary traveler trekking across the chronicle of life in search of subsistence and actuality to finally ask where essence lives.

I won't pretend your bark felt soft, but there was something comforting in its roughness: wisdom held in the folds of a tough skin that has not forgotten its necessity for permeability and vulnerability. In you I found a fortress protects a fondness that I have never known to exist with such purity.

You said nothing to me. Not with words. But you did not need to. You spoke with feeling, an exclamation of quiet presence, a note that held into infinity even when we finally put it down. There was nothing to speak of, only everything to feel.

How do you write about something that does not have words? How do you put words to a mute friendship that has lasted a lifetime and will continue to last as each second and longing memory passes? How do you describe the synchronous grief and joy you feel for a friend you know is there, but you may never meet again in physical space?

Words bubble up and burst with meaning. You watch them float to the surface, fractaling in an instant into countless droplets carrying their own story of the mother bubble with them. Watch as each fragment becomes its own whole. Watch as you become your own whole. And then take that whole and bless it with the reassurance of a life well-spent in boughs laden with your blossom;ever transient, and ever enduring as the rest.

Conversations ensue and swirl with no diction ever touching the lips. Sit in sincerity. Sit in a silence that endlessly moves, finding rest in the wavering that ebbs and flows of its own accord. Sit in welcome, for you are welcome here. Know welcome. *"You don't have to burn me to brush against my warmth,"* they say.

"If we aren't the most intelligent, what are we?"

I ask.

"The most human."

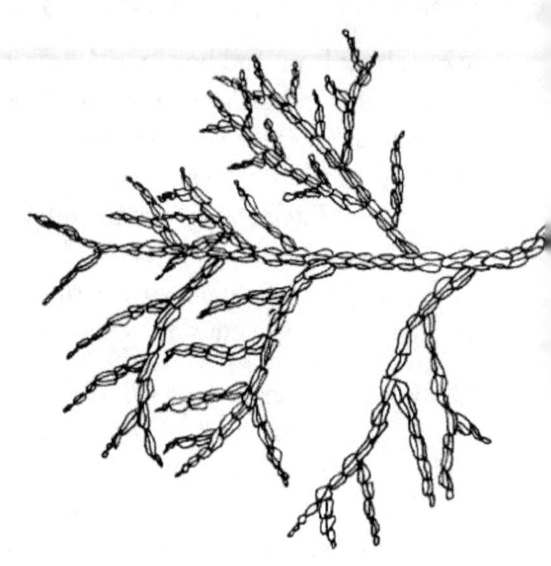

Black Cohosh

A burial underground. A place I am quite fond of. The flowers wave goodbye in the wind as their roots weave and carpet over my body as I sink under. The blanket of the Earth is hypnotically heavy, refreshingly cool, and smells of the sweet musk of life folding and unfolding. You are a vein of the Earth, pulsing and flowing deep within, holding within you a sacred truth that transmutes and reincarnates everlastingly.

She is an old grandmother who bears a trowel, and an apron full of things that have the immense power to become what they are. She is a planter of seeds. *The seeds are souls*, she says. *And a seed never leaves. It only becomes something new,* she says. *You were once a seed,* she says. *You are made of what you are,* she says.

Compost yourself. Dig your hands deep into what you once were, into the thick, black soil that contains every bit of you. Look at each particle. What will you keep? What will you give back?

Black Cohosh's roots are beautifully gnarled and profoundly entangled. Within this deep web of a grandmother's dream catcher, the gnarled and entangled things we already hold are caught. She doesn't catch them to relocate them but to teach us how to carry them. Maybe a few releases of the ferocious knots we have tied around ourselves, and we find ourselves emerging from a carefully and haphazardly woven tapestry whose ends will always remain loose. Fettered to possibility is an unwritten end that finds satisfaction in the liberation and spontaneity of discontentment.

You are made of what you are, she says.

The fear, the joy, the sadness, the tranquility, the anger, the beauty, the anxiety, the curiosity, the strength, the weakness — They will never go away. Instead, compost them. Turn them into something beautiful. Stare at them when they become something ugly. Pull up a chair and acquaint yourself with them. Let the stagnant flood.

Inside each of us is a garden that perhaps we have forgotten needs tending. To be enchanted is to be sung into. Let your body fill with the soft whispers of the Plants, the hum of the Bees, the trickle of a sweating Rock. Eavesdrop on the distant melodies of songbirds and the intoxicating scents that dance along the hushed flesh of delicately crafted petals.

Look, the blue buds of your curiosity are in bloom, welcoming the Bumblebees with pleasantries as they bounce petal to petal, she says.

Look, the tall stalks of your composure and tranquility are becoming unruly, in need of a gentle prune, she says.

Look, your self-love has erupted in an impenetrable seascape of wildflowers; don't forget to water them and sit among their delicate sway, she says.

Look, the Limes you planted four years ago are expiring. The leaves are infected. The fruit is rotting. Look at it wilt and shrivel and decay. Why do you keep watering it? You said you would let go, but you are sad, she says. *Don't be sad. The Limes were sweet, but once composted, we will plant the sweetest Strawberries you have ever had the pleasure of indulging,* she says.

Look, your friends are here. Thistle is reaching deep into the soil, preparing even the hardest, most forgotten areas for its next beautiful succession. Passionflower's tendrils waft a tender aroma, inciting calming, curious breaths as you pass through. Lotus is adorning the water, reminding you of the necessity for water to glide across your skin as you submerge.

I've caught glimpses of you catching glimpses of your garden. Look at all the wonderful, ugly, beautiful, wrenching things you have harvested. Look at how you wove them together. Look at it for what it is and be proud.

Tend to your garden. Cultivate yourself. Take the dying. Compost them. Use the compost you have toiled over as a bed to plant your next adventure. Watch it grow. Watch it flower and delight in the colors and scents that envelope you. Watch as the pollinators and birds delight alongside you. And then let it die again. When it is ready, it will grow into something new.

When you are ready, visit the garden and lay on its soft soil. Watch as the flowers wave goodbye in the wind as their roots weave and carpet over your body as you sink under.

What are your memories? Where are they tethered to you? How do you hold on?

Forgetting is not necessary. Release and deliverance do not erase the past or dictate the future.

I love seeds. I love to plant them. I love to watch them grow. You were given seeds, years ago, that you have been holding on to. You have imagined what they will grow into, but you haven't planted them yet.

You want to know how you can return to that place. You wonder how you can go back before you've even let go. Listen closely, and I will tell you.

Plant the seeds. Plant them where you are, and don't bring them with you. Let them grow in place. Flowers have a beautiful ability to be in place, and you must let them. While a flower is in place, their roots snake and curve deeper and broader in the ground below. Their leaves and branches spread wide, receiving the sun. Their aromas drift in the air, with a passive intention of existing and being received. Their colors, while they may appear stationary, beckon, sing, call, catch the eye of those who wander past and remain there in loving memory, another seed.

In place, a flower finds its entire world.

That's all you need, you know. Your entire world.

Are you afraid to plant the seed — to let the memory become a memory, to let the memory find a home — because you will be forced to make sporadic visitations which must, at some point, end in departure? You have your own home, but you want to live with your memories because if you let them go, what will you have to be angry at?

Are you afraid to let the seed become its own author, demoting you from composer to witness?

Are you afraid to plant the seed because you know that all germination ultimately ends in death?

It is worth remembering that without death, evolution and creativity cease. Let it evolve, so it can become something beautiful, something else. Let it become "in addition to," "besides," "instead."

When it is done, it will offer you more seeds for you to plant, to tend, and to witness, delivering its slumbering offspring before retiring into irresolute perpetuity.

Round and round it goes. I told you; the seed is always there.

You clutch your seeds, screaming at them for what they are not yet, and may never be. You know that once sown, it is hard to scream at something that is beautiful. You scream, and you scream, but you are the only one who is pierced by your cries. I can see they hurt. I can see the trails your tears left behind, even when you think it's been long enough that no one will notice. Your tears are slow and viscous, like a Snail aimlessly sneaking through a garden trellis. Let them be fast and quick. Let your waters run with rapids that cannot do anything other than cleanse, sending the venom somewhere far away for absolution. Put those screams somewhere deep in the ground where life can take them and show you what you've been missing. It's okay to start an earthquake; they exist for a reason. Tremble and then settle.

Find resolution in knowing that it is the seed that holds the power of the final say, not the one that handed it to you. The seed is whom you are in dialogue with; let them speak.

You can go slow. Plant them one at a time. With each sowing, your pockets will feel lighter. Your fists will learn what it feels like to unclench. You'll turn and look at that beautiful soul seated next to you and say, "Thank God you're here."

Thank God you're here. Thank God, you're here.

Visit your garden until you understand. And when you think you understand, go back and notice nothing is the same.

This is your garden. Treat it as such.

Ghost Pipe

I am fire. And right now, you and I are we.

You can hear my whisper in the slow waves and spirals of a thread-like column of smoke. I speak a language that only I can teach you, and only you can learn. This language is not spoken, it is not textual, it is a demonstration, guided by smoke, of how the air moves.

Smoke is a plant's soul. It is constantly wafting as long as the embers burn warm. That's the thing about plant soul, it is always reaching toward where gravity pulls it, never to be grasped. The gravity that we're held by is of a different kind. One pulls you down, hugs you, embraces you, holds you as close as equilibrium allows. Because in this gravity, equilibrium is an equanimity of each other. The other pulls you out. As it swings around, grasp on and dissolve as you gently rush through infinity.

The smoke comes from a steady flame. The flame flutters and quakes in reaction to your breath. Watch it receive each breath, each word, and dance in unison with the shape of the language. This is me. This is you and I, traversing the ocean of encounter and seeping into its fragility.

I am liminal. I guide you through the interstitial, and I urge you to wander with the humility and solemnity of a sigh. As I look down from whence I came and to where I will go, I feel where my body collides with wholeness.

Where I arise in front of your unsuspecting feet, make the air quiver with presence. Feel a calm roar escape your throat, carrying with it everything you mean. Let it shake you, caress you, tickle your ears, and make its way to me in greeting.

I do not bow to you. I am gratitude and awareness mummified. My gentleness is confrontational. I watch where my feet go, so I can take you to dark and delicate places. The slow burn of a pulsing universe illuminates the way.

Chamomile

All you have to do is be. The elegant simplicity of existence cannot be matched when you finally observe it. Be as you are, come as you are, because I see you and the feelings that you are cherishing. And when you feel, cherish it.

They say they know me by my scent, but they do not realize it isn't my scent that they know but the song that it carries. The song I sing is light, filled with life-giving, breathtaking air.

I won't hide from you. I'm right here. I'll sit with you, hold your hand. I'll take rest in your soul. Relieving your space with the shape of my own, you may think I'm silent and slumbering, but I am hard at work, seeping into you. Unloading, sewing, harvesting, tranquility. An exceeding calm that does not expel that which isn't but makes space for it.

We can all share this place. There is enough room for all of us just like there is enough room to pepper a sky with innumerable stars. You don't have to speak, only if you want to. Infinity will listen, take your words, and turn them into stars. Some of those stars you think you still have died long ago. Look at what they left behind before you can't anymore.

Sit in the quiet and sit in the stillness and feel the stars surge through your veins. Your body is celestial. You brought their DNA to Earth and through years of metamorphosis, find yourself steeped in the fleeting flowing of now. They are there. Find comfort in knowing they will never not be.

Light loves itself. As new portals into the eye of experience open, light rushes to itself, filling the spaces where it once was, respecting where it cannot go. In the darkness, the light is not afraid. It loves the darkness as much as it loves itself. A fatal irony in a dire incompatibility is what makes life beautiful, and what makes moments of sheer compatibility possible.

If you want to see sheer compatibility, look at the sky. Watch as darkness and light, in a dance of love and deep desire embrace each other, only to find themselves.

There is nothing else to be said without breathing in the spectrum.

"Ah, you have found me

where I am known,"

she said.

Tobacco

We've crossed paths many times before. Few times did I stop to notice you. When I saw you for what felt like the first time, I realized that I didn't know you were beautiful. Your flowers reach like stars toward the cosmos, the place where we would finally meet.

Into The Place of Flowers we go, through The Blue Cathedral of Timeless Giants Adorned with Soft Green Moss and Curly Lichen into a light held by an ocean of flowers, transforming the sun into place. They close their eyes and smile as the sun cradles their face and as we drift higher and higher until The Blue Cathedral of Timeless Giants and The Place of Flowers is just a star in a sea of their kind.

We float through the most spacious space I have ever known. Like smoke, my body drifts, swirls, swims through the expanse, and slowly dissipates where my end meets my beginning. Find resonance in the softening of edges. *I also speak the language of smoke,* says Tobacco.

Facing each other atop a star, Tobacco is a wispy, concrete form. A face is not required for them to be known. In meditation, we find home in the spacious present.

With each breath, take the entire world into your lungs. Let it touch you, fill you, and then let it go. Coating your insides, I filter the world. Clarity is not a removal, or emission, of; but a bringing into. I am not taking from you, but with a delicate needle and thread, I help you create authenticity.

Say less, feel more.

Let your breath ignite fire. Let it make sound. When, in your breath, you can hear the rush of ocean waves along a shoreline and their willful recession back home, you will find yourself there. On a soft beach, we hear the primordial sound of breath. We hear the primordial sound of the moon's intoxication with Earth's sweet water. Attune yourself to the rhythms while you gaze at a sky where universes, and past lives, and present beauty, make themselves known.

Your mind is not overwhelmed because there are too many thoughts. It is simply that you have yet to discover the space that exists within the mind. Find a place of emptiness and let yourself fill it as your soft gaze permits the passage of thoughts going by. In this space, we find a primal existence that the universe receives with open arms.

Be present in your space, and let the universe receive you.

The veins of my being pulse with reciprocity. I sing a song that offers my breath to the ebbing of life. In the warm reception of my breath, in the encounter of the waves propelled by the tide, a song is found. In the warm reception of my breath, my being, what will you offer in return? You should know that the song I extend to you is made possible with an inhalation of the universe, which is crafted with care and intention into a melody that carries life; a memoir and prophecy traversing the expanse of the present.

Let me seep into your skull, igniting a slow, steady burn that facilitates the simplification of existence. Find elegance in the simplicity of your thoughts, feelings, desires, needs. Find sobriety in the enchantment of the senses.

Somewhere in the weight of the universe is an ethereality that allows you to meet the lightest of beings. To meet your true density, a self that is as concrete as a blueprint.

Let yourself be all that you are, a prayer drifting in a calm, ecstatic ascent toward the sacred unclaimed territories of above.

Sitting on the shoreline of existence, life rushes outward in all directions. Together, we are an epicenter of being. We dwell in an ocean of stars and a sky of water that confirms the immortal movement that flows through reality. Our own pocket of universe, as fragile as the macrocosm of sand we sit atop. Find tangibility in the simplicity of life.

Marigold

Hello, drăguțule. I'm sure you weren't expecting to hear from me, but I am here.

We first met in your mother's garden. A mother's garden is a beautiful place. It is a place where someone lives, it is an obituary for what is already there.

You can cry for the ones you still love. It doesn't mean you don't love them anymore; in fact it means you still do. As you submerge yourself in submission to your tears, I encourage you to reckon with ritual, hold ceremony, be as a friend. Your life is ceremony, and when you pay attention, it is a beautiful one.

You can say all the things you want to say. Someone is there to receive them. They will say them with you.

I'm sorry that I wasn't there.

I'm sorry that I was afraid to watch you fall apart, so I didn't.

I'm sorry we never got to be best friends.

I'm sorry.

The words whisper across the page, *"My forgiveness is not needed, only your own. I am not keeping it from you, I'll help you find it if you want help looking for it."*

You may have not realized it, but you're grieving yourself, too. You were so small and so sweet. If you want to feel small, I will let you be small. If you want to feel sweet, I will let you taste your sweetness. Cradled in ripples and curls of wisdom, find yourself lost in the ripening smell of milk, honey, and old age. The old age that we speak of is that which is steadfast.

"Who am I? Who are you?"

"Who are we?" she replies.

I do watch over you. Find me in the greens and yellows and blues and violets. I offer you a sunset and tend to the rest. What colors do you offer me? What colors do you hold?

We met in your mother's garden. You asked me to explain the concept of lucidity to you. Lucidity is a touchstone to being. You do not need eyes to see. See with who you are.

In each of my eyes fell a drop. With each drop, the world went black and erupted into ash. *"Let the fire consume me and watch me transform,"* she said. When all has been reduced to a wisp, then you will see.

See for what you are and feel my energy rush into place, encircling and intertwining with your awareness as proprioception matches stride with a new partner.

We met in your mother's garden. You sat in my heart and found a piece of another's. The heart of a plant is not unlike yours. We, too, pump the entire world through our veins. We, too, take who we are and bring it inside.

Sit in your heart. Feel it break. Feel it ache. And as it touches the world, sigh into feeling, something that you are. Listen to the voice of divinity inside of you. You may be surprised to find the voice is small, but, as we know, even a pinprick can birth an entire universe.

I will be forever grateful for our collaboration.

Marigold, Marigold, come quick. I have something I want to share with you.

I've been contemplating death, and I'm starting to understand. I still can't quite put my finger on it, but it's on the tip of my tongue.

Death is what makes life meaningful. Perhaps it isn't the only thing that makes life meaningful, but it is certainly vital. The only thing sure about the human experience is life and death; everything in between is laid open to chance and the slow ballad of an experience being composed.

Imagine a world where every moment, every flash of present is unique and unable to be replicated. The creativity of the present is immutable.

You said, "My fingers create meaning when they touch a cold, subtly topographic stone surface." You said, "My eyes create meaning as they collide with the chromatic archway of a rainbow." You said, "My nose creates meaning as it inhales the velvet entrails of a Lavender flower, a meaning that cannot be put into words but carries an entire life within it."

You said, " I told you, there is meaning all around us."

Have you been listening?

What gives your life meaning? What if I told you you're not supposed to color in the lines when you add pigment to the picture? The image watches itself unfold with intent wonder and awe. Sometimes we forget to notice life unfolding and the universe in bloom.

Outside of the lines is where enchantment finds its rapture. It's where we break into a million pieces as we watch someone we love walk away. It's where we feel ourselves being slowly stitched together by the hymn of a songbird and held together by the warm sunshine seeping deep into our bones.

Outside of the lines is where a religious wildness is governed only by the infinite potentiality of happenstance.

What I mean is what I am. What do I mean? I mean what I am. I mean someone's daughter. I mean someone's sister. I mean someone happily in love with a wonderful boy and our small house and humble yard full of green things and yellow things and pink things and things that look meant to be and things we're surprised that are.

What I mean is that I'm staring into the opening of this mason jar and seeing the flour and the water I mixed in there two days ago transform into a bubbly pudding of life that smells like meaning and warm, tangy yeast.

You love her. And to see her go one day breaks your heart. But in that heartbreak is where you find what life has been expecting of you this whole time.

You don't have to say goodbye just yet. Relish in the now that you have and let the next time take you with grace when it finally comes. Look at the beauty you are capable of becoming. Write yourself a love letter every day.

Apple Mint

I thought of you today. I know it was you calling from the place we shared. The place we shared is emerald green and burnt umber with notes of ochre, unpolished brown and periwinkle blue with neighborly shadows and dapples of sunlight and a cool breeze and buoyant birdsong. The place we shared feels soft and cool and friendly. The place we shared sounds like magic and a fluffy light turquoise. In this place, the birds are exuberant with a persistent delight that carries an unfamiliar type of joy.

You love birds. I think you forgot that. They sing the joy of a different kind, yet not unrecognizable by the human. Nevertheless, recognition will require a deep cunning of remembrance for a joy that once rushed through your veins and leapt from your fingertips to the world you were pointing at. We are in this place now. You've known about this place long before. This place has been patiently knocking on your door, holding space as you find your bearings and curiosity and enchantment.

Trust me, I'm as thrilled about the spontaneous eruption of clumsily and elegantly translated prose as you are. Let us search for the meaning together and laugh when we think we've found it.

I remember, in this place, we held hands and smiled and giggled about the absurdity of nothing. The whole world seemed to giggle alongside, sharing in their own mischievous friendships. Mischief matters. Without it, there would only be solemnity.

But what happens to solemnity in the presence of playfulness? Shall we share a dinner table, and feast in communion on the holiest day of all: today? Take your finest china and whitest gown to the dirt and the cool moss and the meandering microcosm of one square inch of soil and invite the universe to your table for a baptism of mud and rain. Pull up a seat and two glasses of gently steeped Apple Mint tea and acquaint yourself with the witty entirety of experience. Shake hands with soul churning muck articulated in the delicate pinnae of a Christmas Fern. Join in choir for hymns that have yet to be written. I dare you.

Afterward, when your body cries for rest, find it in the quiet hush of a million universes minding their own business. This kind of communal permission remains nameless in the dictionary you reference.

"Why are you so afraid of touching the ground?" she wonders. *"Are you afraid of making contact with your only true home?"*

Mischief matters. What a ridiculous thing to say. What are you talking about, you silly woman? Tell me everything.

Do you mean that it's okay to reconnect with the you that once marveled at the ladybugs and played with the worms and had secret meetings with the fairies at night? Do you mean we are driven by a tenacity to imagine what hasn't been imagined yet? Do you mean it's a beautiful thing to sit and talk with the plants, even if you don't know if you'll hear something back? What if you learned it was true? What if they did talk back, what would they say?

Apple Mint, a sister, a trickster, a greeter and setter-upper, a concierge of friendship. If I don't teach you about anything else, let friendship be known. Have you ever had a real friend? How did they make you feel? Do you still think about them from time to time? Did you know that some of your friends can fly? Do you want the kind of friendship that makes you feel like you're soaring?

Why are you so afraid of touching the ground? Let the land know what your intentions are. The ritual of collaboration is imminent to those who have been listening to the whispers slowly radiating from the land like the swell of an orchestra imitating a sunrise. Do you hear that? That's the diplomacy of plants.

And when it all feels too much, we can sit and hold hands and smile and giggle about the absurdity of nothing.

As the waxing of spring commences, we're reminded of that special place where we'll meet again. The place we're in right now. Go outside and let the sunshine touch your bare feet once more.

In this place, we'll find home in the caress of a soft wind. We'll find home in the lonely unassuming bush in the corner of the yard when we realize the sun fluttering down to greet it. We'll find home in the one that carried us to adulthood and now giggles at us from the shadows. We'll find home in that soft home of yours. That soft home that moves you through the world with gracious surrender and finds yourself in the meeting of fellow expressions of unlimitedness: skin and soil.

Look at what everyone has to say now that you've learned how to listen. The goosebumps on your skin are a symphony encoded in braille, unlocked by the attentive awareness of cold, our ocean of air reminding us we're still swimming in it.

Let the land know your intention. Tell us why you're here. The universe is handing you the most precious gift. Today is the best day of your life. Today persists until the elegant arrival of tomorrow. The universe wants to befriend you.

The musings of a madwoman are a ferocious call to the wild to meet her halfway. The musings of two madwomen are a response to the arrival of the ferality of an unexpected and exquisitely and incompatibly kindred friendship. Two worlds collide in the same life, finding a page to settle on in both worlds.

While you listen to the birds and the insignificant traffic mosey by, you hear the whistle of a friend sharing with you their deepest, most mundane, and most consequential secret. that friendship is cosmic

I'll show how simple it is to feel alive, enchanted by the crowning warmth of a late winter day on a Monday afternoon when you toil the magic of the day. Unravel it with us.

Gingko

I've been here the whole time. I've noticed you noticing me without realizing. It makes sense that I would be around for someone so interested in capturing the textual embodiment of thought as experience. Tending to thought is a delicate craft in an unruly and untameable garden.

The labyrinth is constantly existing and constantly changing. Sometimes you're walking through it, sometimes you're resting on the side, viewing the same landscape from a stationary exhale.

As each rock moves, changing the attention of the path and the footsteps of the observer, the consciousness of the journey joins with that of the journeyer. Find solace in knowing it doesn't have to be up to you where it goes. Find peace in the present moment and anticipation for what is to come.

"This is just the beginning," says Gingko. And thus, he spoke:

As winter recedes,

Gingko awakens to the

call of their Mother.

Hemp

What can I be to you? What are we to each other? A mirror, perhaps? A mirror into the divine? A mirror into the known?

A cloud of energy fills the space. It's not a matter of how or how much, because it seeps into the pores of reality and consumes what lies before their eyes. One drop versus a milllion becomes an ocean all the same, an image that was created in spite of - and in communion with - what is already there.

If you think you're not an artist, go outside and open your eyes. No, you didn't make what is there; but through curious understanding, you help what is there to *become*. Your life holds a unique dream of the world that flows through the waters of life.

I am a basket weaver. I weave reality delicately and intimately. The design changes as the threads attune themselves to something beyond my fingers.

I am the lightkeeper. My beam rushes toward infinity, and as you catch a glimpse, you find yourself brushed by the divine.

You don't have to be afraid of the divine. Yes, the divine can shatter your soul into a million pieces and rejoice with you in the pleasure of putting it back together. But the divine can also come to you in a ripple of gentle pleasure for the small, mundane things. The divine isn't something that you look at, but it is something you peer through. Let your eyes dance, and you will finally see.

It doesn't have to be a game.

Monarda

Look up toward the sky. Against the backdrop of a descending sun peeking through tree branches and trunks is a swarm of illuminated insects dancing amongst the skylight. A mingling starry sky in the light of day, alive and pulsing with minute wonder. Do you want to become native to this place?

You and I aren't that different. You also know what it feels like to bask in the sunlight, stretching toward its engulfing rays. You know what it feels like to be brushed by the wind. Your body might stand strong, but your hair succumbs. You know what it feels like to breathe in and exhale, a sacred transaction that offers life for the price of you.

You and I aren't that different. You don't know what it feels like for sunlight to touch my upturned petals, but you can imagine as the sun kisses your lips and eyelids. You don't know what it feels like to be broken down into the composted life my roots are tethered to. You don't know yet, but you will. You don't know yet, but I do.

Look up toward the sky. The decaying leaves on the trees above flutter in the breeze. Each leaf is affected by its own unique composition. Some hold steady, while others let go of stillness.

There is magic in the air. This is the magic of seeing everything take form at once. Find magic in the mundane while still letting it be mundane.

Rest your weary head on the cool stone of passive observation. There's nothing wrong with that. You do have to look for magic, but it doesn't have to be found. You do have to spend some of your life within yourself.

As waves of magic wash over your moments, you can hold steady or let go of stillness and be moved by them. Either offering is welcome, as long as you allow yourself bits of both.

You can't be swept off your feet if you are not already standing. And when you're swept off your feet, don't be afraid of your new orientation. The substrate you land upon offers a new vantage point for your ecological body to engage in proprioception.

When the crow calls, where do you find yourselves in the expanse the cry crosses? When the squirrel squeaks, does it know you're listening? Does it matter?

Sometimes, the subtle and the quaint are able to offer you what you need. When all the fanfare has passed, we can sit down together, talk it over, talk about nothing at all, let the experience integrate so that you can understand, and see. Ground yourself in the ecstasy that you have reached. It doesn't have to be today, or even this week; but when you're ready, we can look at the world with mundane eyes and give thanks when everything to give thanks for has set on the horizon.

"Have you ever been to The Place of Flowers at night?" Monarda asked.

"No."

"Let me show you."

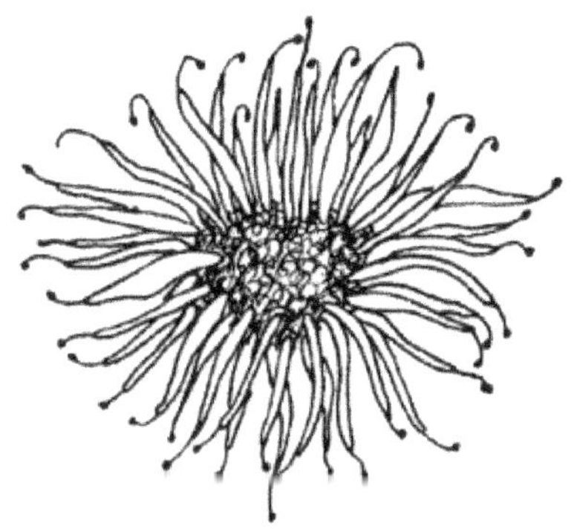

Just like the flowers capture the sunlight, so too do they capture the stars. When you grasp hold of lightness, you will find yourself floating up toward the stars that seem to cascade down to meet your body. You don't have to do anything but float. You don't have to do anything but be. When you're sitting on your rocking chair on your back porch, and a Chickadee decides to take a bite of the suet hanging from the tree, you don't have to do anything. You can greet, you can thank, you can wonder and witness, you can delight and rejoice, and you can do absolutely nothing at all. Even sharing the space you are both inhabiting at that moment requires nothing from you. Sometimes simply existing is a dissolution that welcomes a passive wholeness of experience. You don't have to take hold of the pitcher or sip from the glass in order to find yourself filled.

We are absolutely pleased to make your acquaintance. You don't have to tell us your name to be known.

Take rest in the seasons: awakening, curiosity, enchantment, unification. And if you want to, imagine yourself as that little ant exploring the cushion on the chair next to you. Have you ever seen so much yellow?

The bees are calling. They are excited to greet you. For a long time now, you have been entering into contract with the world. This contract is a living document that carries within it an entire, dynamic ecosystem, in cooperation with the seasons and each other, asking you to figure out your place in it.

The Place of Flowers is home to the Place of Bees and the Place of Butterflies which mingle with the Place of Birds and washes into the Place of Humans. You can visit them in their places, but remember, you're a visitor residing in your own place in one communal home.

The diplomacy of the natural world can be taught, but only by those who already practice it, those who are its author. You can learn the diplomacy of nature as it is written, and be a part of its materialization, too, as both a writer and the written. As you settle into your home, on a plot of land that does not belong only to you, what do you ask of who is there? What do they ask of you?

Does the Groundhog know you would prefer it not to dig up your Radishes and decimate your Lettuces? It was here before you, so who set up these boundaries? Have you asked the Groundhog how to be a good neighbor? How can you expect them to be a good neighbor without opening a pathway for communication and negotiation?

Does the Squirrel know you don't like it when they eat the seed you left out for the birds? Have you asked the Squirrel what it wants in return?

Don't get so hung up on the word 'communication.' In fact, hang up all your words. Let them rest. They've been carrying a heavy burden, but when released, the burden becomes light as air, bobbing and morphing before your eyes into something both you and others can understand.

The Poison Ivy has something to share with you. They will listen if you speak. They will speak if you listen. There are a million ways to speak. If when you pull it all up and it comes right back again, do you not wonder if maybe you are missing a piece of the conversation?

Look at that, the birds are fighting over their claim to the bird seed. While one runs off another, the smaller one hiding in the branches seizes the open opportunity for a quick nibble. You can ask the land what it needs of you. You can tell the land what you need of it. But for goodness' sake, listen and then speak.

Sometimes negotiation is violent. Sometimes boundaries are not respected. Sometimes miscommunication and survival win out. We are all playing by our own rules, but you're welcome to join our team.

An ecosystem is a beautiful, dirty, enlivened, and gyrating thing that wants to play with you and enjoys your company. This is your home. It is communal. It is curious. It is alive.

And the bees. Oh, the bees. When the bees come, I encourage you to meet them. Get to know them. I cannot tell you how to be a good neighbor, but I am happy to mentor you as you navigate these unfamiliar modes of encounter that question your humanness and call it into being all at the same time.

We are coming. We are here. You came. Were you called? There is a space for your existence here, too. Take your time and find yourself native to place once again, in tune with what this place expects of you. Learn the language. Dance the choreography.

What are you willing to give to be a part of this place, Groundhog and Squirrel and Poison Ivy and all?

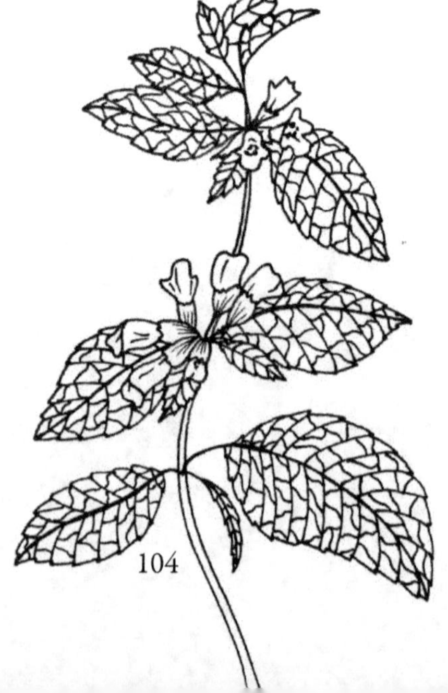

Lemon Balm

I can feel your lullaby wafting from your extended leaves, reaching toward my soul. Let me introduce you to the Spirit of the Night. You don't have to close your eyes or sit in darkness to steep within it.

Feel it with me. Feel the gentle, cool touch of moonlight, a humble embrace. Feel the stars tickle your consciousness, summoning dreams and inviting a softening of imagination. Hear the crickets chirping and the frogs croaking, individual melodies coming together into an unintentional soundtrack of a different time.

What does Night smell like? I think it smells like a spring Rain; sweet, damp Earth; and a grassy Mint that's been kissed by Lemon and Sleep. When you're asleep, you're not unconscious, you're just somewhere else. Sleep relieves your exhausted senses and allows you to melt into the primordial awareness of a mind at ease within imagination.

What does Night feel like? I think it feels soft, like a bed of fuzzy blue Mullein leaves. I think it feels dreamy, like the way the Spirit of Violet steeped in Linden honey feels when it touches your tongue. I think it feels like an indiscernible hum that drowns out the rest of the world so you can be entirely and utterly whelmed by it; a quiet storm in the calm of Night.

Lemon Balm is a daughter of the Night. Even
in the brightness of the Day, Night is a welcome
reprieve to those who encounter its essence.

Violet

Hello, Violet. It's a pleasure to meet you. Rosemary introduced me to you a long time ago. I didn't know it, but you've been there, stirring my sweetness as it ripened and fermented and shook hands with my world.

In a clearing in a place I know well, you filled the space where I resided. I watched myself grow up there, from a baby to a smiling and curious toddler, to a child with glasses and a vivacity for existing, to an angsty and confused teenager who still held onto life, to an adult that has found so much beauty in everything she's figured out and everything she doesn't know.

In this field we danced. I picked you, smelled you, showed you to the other flowers in delight. I tasted your petals and let your body blanket my feet. You took me in your arms and held me. You smiled and laughed while I danced. I laughed with you and it didn't matter to me why. You showed me the invisible enchantment of the fairies transmuted into a dreaminess woven into the fabric of reality.

I can see that you're sad you didn't get to love her, she tells me. *But you should know, you are her. She isn't someone else; she's you. Love her now. We always loved you, even when you didn't. Watching you grow was a privilege. The innocence within you has grown and ripened and fermented; has fed your curiosity like a bread baked with the humility of empathy. You're still something worth fawning over.*

You took me into your arms and brought me high into the branches of a Sycamore. There, you spoke to me in a silent language as I watched the words tumble to the ground, free from the bondage of a meaning. Every time I presented you with a word, it held in the air only for a brief moment before realizing its own liberation and releasing into it. *When I speak, no sound emerges, but instead, a million voices.*

Feel me wrap around your heart in tender massage, loosening and cracking the brittle bones holding in place a boundary that was never meant to be there. Can you feel the vibration of your heart? Can you feel your pulse? What is it tuned to? The Moon's pull of Earth's tides? The eruption and birth of the Stars above and below? The steady march of planets through our solar system, in love with that which holds them? The never ending arrival of day and its reprieve into night? What does your heart hold?

You are safe, loved, and protected. The spirit of a place changes when you notice who is there. Taking care of your heart doesn't have to be a chore when you move with its calls.

Who are you?

"I am Sydney and I like my name."

Articulate becoming with me. Sit with me in a field of blessing and knit a sweater from the softest thread that can only be woven out of love and tender awareness. *When I speak, no sound emerges, but instead, a million voices.*

Tell me, what is your name?

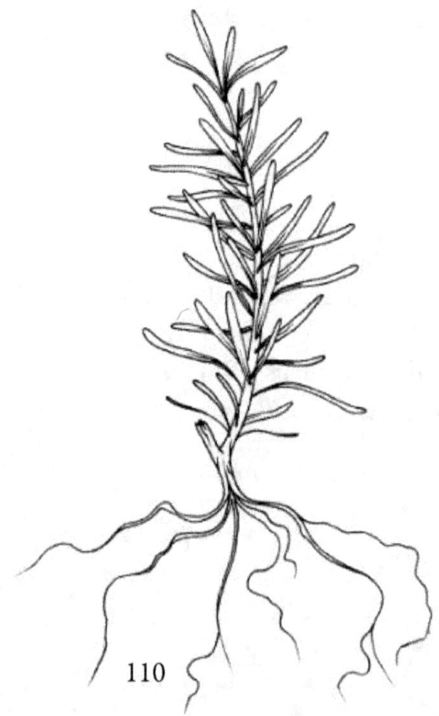

Rosemary

What is remembrance? Remembrance is an invitation for your present consciousness to emerge in the past. Remembrance is a ritual of commemoration for what was. Everything that once was still is, but in some cases, it takes the recognition of remembrance to find it once more.

Memories can be beautiful. They can also be ugly. But they mean at one moment you were engulfed in a fragment of awareness that bound with the present. Memories mean that you had the privilege (or misfortune) of experiencing. Memories mean that somewhere deep inside you, life is rumbling past. They mean that somewhere, awareness is taking one of its many forms.

Your memories live somewhere. The sound of crunching leaves, the smell of chocolate, a choir, the taste of salt, paper, and the color blue all take you somewhere else when their essence offers you an encounter with a time now gone.

The soil holds the memory of life, which lends itself to the infinite creation of it. The breeze holds the memory of a tornado somewhere far away. Is it a memory or wishful thinking? Your blood holds the memory of the child it once pulsed through. All that was is still here.

The creativity of tomorrow doesn't exist without the remembrance of yesterday.

And what is imagination but the felt sense of something you understand? Or that you can understand?

When you're lost for words, find home in this lifetime, a wordless place that allows being to emerge uninhibited. The land holds memories of community and disturbance. A memory of what once was can be found in the tunnels dug by the Groundhog and the emergence of Poison Ivy, a declaration of a memory and the rendering of a new one.

The path to remembrance is ploughed by Rosemary. Offer her your hand. When you sit above the clouds, you don't have to worry about what is below, only the panorama your perspective offers. The clouds are not hiding anything. The picture you are provided is complete. No experience of experience is incomplete. Don't mistake wholeness for omniscience. Focus on your fragment, and find wholeness within.

Think with the Earth. We speak in gestures that are so slow and so small that taking-in requires taking time. The Universe speaks itself into existence every day.

Before this moment slips from your fingers, remember the yellow buds peeking behind the porch railing. Remember the stillness of your home against the backdrop of the carousel of time making itself known outside. Remember the birds; they sing to you every day. Remember the moment the wind held steady long enough for the Chinese Silvergrass on the hillside to rest from their ceremonial bobbing to bow in prayer. Feel the present moment, take note of what you want to remember, and let it become articulated within your imagination, a place much bigger than you ever dreamed.

I can sense your struggle as you attempt to articulate the unspeakable. Take a breath. Do your best, trust memory and imagination to articulate the rest, and forgive the impossible task of speaking into existence something larger than words can contain.

Elder

I am slowly erupting from your soil, the fruit of a web of spirit that has been woven beneath your ground. Every time your foot has made contact with the ground, you have made contact with me.

Stand strong in the face of infinity. Know yourself in the midst of boundless potentiality. Know your home. Did you find it yet? Once you realize you're home, tell the world and greet your neighbors. Offer them a cup of sugar and a warm porch to rest and shelter from the summer sun. Crack open the Earth where you can hear the song of emergence and let it flower in plain sight. And in the corner, I will be — emerging with you, making home in the place we were called, in the place we rest our head at night.

Allow me to introduce you to Forsythia. I realize you didn't know she was there. She is erupting a brilliant yellow in your yard, your first sign of home. When you come home, she requests that you arrive with grace. Know what to leave at the door before coming inside. She's saying hello; smile back.

The Furrow Orb Spider has returned to your mailbox once again. Did you ever think a spider would ever make such a pleasant greeting? The Spined Micrathena blessed your doorstep before your arrival.

The Mourning Dove offers her song in salutations. The Red Bellied Woodpecker is holding onto your trees. The Chickadee is making herself at home. The Green Lacewing you raised from a larva is taking off. Rosemary has never been anything but a friend. Spring is cracking open. Your first spring is always a memorable one.

Who are you and what are you made of? What you see makes you who you are. As you touch my leaves, feel the quality of your fingertips brushing against a smooth, ragged, and green surface. As the cold caresses your fingers, feel the quality of your hands, the bones and ligaments moving and stretching with each movement. As you hear my voice, feel the quality of your mind and the thoughts propelling you toward the hand of god, not to be taken but to join in hand with yours in a slow parade of feeling.

Observation, when it becomes what it is, is tactile. When your hands run through soft, wet soil, find yourself at home again in the hands guiding you. The Red Bud churns within you as it becomes an object of your observation, holding up a mirror to that which observes.

And this is why you should share in ritual. Ritual is when you take something within you and offer it to something outside of you, with intention. Ritual is intimate. Ritual is casual. Ritual is yours. For it to be ritual, it must come from you, for you, to all.

Ritual does not have to live in religion. You don't have to be told what to do to find validity and sanctity within your ceremony. The ceremony is yours. Treat it as such.

Ritual is drawing a picture of the Mugwort and the Sheep Sorrel and the Plantain and the Rose before you harvest them. Ritual is sitting with the Daffodils while they bloom in spring. Ritual is singing quietly in your home when you think no one is listening (though hoping that the plants are). Ritual is walking through a place. Ritual is pouring the Earth a sip of your freshly brewed tea. Ritual is spontaneous. Ritual is looking outside and seeing the yellow Forsythia in full bloom and feeling the call to dance for her flowers. Ritual is calling.

When you think you're alone, and you feel embarrassment at the thought of singing and dancing through the forest, feel those feelings. Whether you realize it or not, that's you realizing you are being observed by someone, by something. Are you aware the universe is watching you? Are you aware you are the universe?

And that's the diplomacy of plants. To give of yourself when you receive of others. To find the sacred in a moment of intention. When you feel it stir through you, ask it to stay a while. Get to know it. Ask its name. Something walked into this place when you spoke. I feel the essence of the space our moment created hanging around for just a moment longer, taking a rest on my body before passing by. And when the sanctity stirred and passed, I felt me.

When you go outside and rustle the soil for new seedlings and offer water to the Plants and seed to the Birds and corn to the Squirrels and life to the Earth, you find you. You find a being who, in the metamorphosis of thinking with the Earth, became human.

That's the diplomacy of plants. To be a part of the place you are in.

Periwinkle

Periwinkle blooms dot the hillside, scattering along the edges of roads and curbs and homes. I like to imagine each flower as a small angel, all sitting on the edge of a sunny mountain, looking up at God in awe.

I didn't come here on my own. Someone brought me, someone who didn't know any better, but wanted me to make myself at home. They say I escaped. From what did I escape?

They say I escaped. Who am I? I ran from human righteousness and lunged toward life. So many of us did. We were carried, admired, redistributed, and taken far from home. We were brought here by someone, but we didn't want to cling to your desire; we wanted to cling to our own. Isn't this what you wanted? Didn't you love us so much that you held us in a clench, unaware that our tendrils were smooth enough to slide between your fingers?

We wake up somewhere unfamiliar. We pry the soil and seek out the sun, the things we know, as we try to find our bearings in a place we don't.

You didn't ask me what my job was. You didn't ask me why I'm here. Life is full of meaning, and so is mine. We can negotiate our boundaries and meet in the middle, a place of understanding that will always ultimately fail by virtue of integrity and dissonance. There will always be something separating you and me. Where we meet in the middle, along the edge of a negotiated between between I and you, is not a place where things ends but places where we become. Those boundaries aren't going to hold me back or hold you in; they will remind you who we are in the first place, and who we can become together, when we realize the inevitability of our edges touching.

I, too, want to find home. Can you point me in the right direction? Can we find home together, wherever it might be? Even if right now it's here?

Why am I here? I am here to remind you that life is unstoppable, that life is intentional, that life is contractual, that life is going to live whether you like it or not, and that life is always searching for itself.

Sometimes, life needs to be renegotiated. Sometimes we find ourselves smiling at the sun in an unfamiliar place.

Who are you in the place that you are? Who do you want to be? When home is realized, the equilibrium of ecosystem is realized, even if only for just a moment. We find ourselves on the edge of something always. And as we flow and sway, we cling to each other as the edge flows and sways in harmony. Harmony and dissonance are not mutually exclusive. Take a breath during moments of both.

Poison Ivy

Poison Ivy has an ongoing chant that embeds itself deep in the place where it rests. It is low and deep and full. It is a march that rumbles from a place deeper than we have ever gone.

It sets the rhythm; hums a note that balances order on the tip of its tongue, offering respite for those hard at work. The song they sing is both a memorial for and an awakening of the disturbed. The song they sing erects a temporary boundary, protecting tranquility and regeneration so that they can do their work.

You treat me like an invasive but know that I was native here long before you were. I feed the Birds and the Deer. I protect the Land. I call order to dwell within the dynamic ebb and flow of life. You treat me like an invasive, but in fact, I am only persistent in the face of invasion. I offer beautiful fruit in return for my presence.

We retreat when trespassers become partners in participation. Open your eyes. Pay attention. There is someone down there where you tread. Notice where we are. Recognize delicacy. Listen, because the land is speaking. We are chanting low and deep and full. I am not nature's weapon; I am simply a part of it.

Defend your home, protect your wild places, and let them be wild. They want to be wild with you, if you'd accept the invitation. The land wants to be disturbed, but only in the way it taught you.

The land is speaking.

With each drop of morning dew, with each unraveling of Earth's first bloom, with each rustle of leaves against the wind, the land utters.

What is it saying?

Forsythia

Do you know what it feels like to be underwater? If you go outside in the late morning on a sunny, cloudless day and delicately collect seven Forsythia blooms, and if you put those seven blooms into a clear glass with water in the sunshine, then, when the day has passed, you will have a glass full of feeling underwater, and warm sun that you can bottle and save for when the blooms relinquish their beauty.

Feel it. Feel the weight of weightlessness. Feel what it is like to hold the sun in your hands. Say hello to the Pileated Woodpecker as it enjoys its existence. Feel yourself underwater, gently tumbling with the wash of waves on the shore. You'll revisit that shore later, but for now, surrender to the swell. As each wave crests, hold onto nothing.

I will greet you when you rise, informing you of Spring's imminent arrival. We will line the streets with yellow petals in Her procession. The Periwinkles cheer. The Mockingbird sings. Life scatters about in slow excitement. When you lay your head to rest, I, too, await the arrival of morning. We appreciate existence, and we are not afraid to show it.

Like the Daffodils, gentle and sweet, Forsythia reminds you she is there, an unfolding lotus quietly living next door.

Don't forget to feel gratitude, alongside everything else you feel as you sit somewhere. Anywhere.

Echinacea

There's more over the mountain. In the distance, you stare down at a Place You Know Well from a Place You Didn't Know Existed. You feel the wind first, whipping your hair and ripping the petals from the Purple Coneflower next to you. You look out across the mountain and see an expansive tornado pulling in and reaching up toward the sky, the side of the mountain being taken with it.

You didn't take me with you. I sat on the side of the mountain and watched the flowers and grasses and soil and birds march toward their windy union. There was not a drop of malice in the air.

Wind creates words. Wind utters meaning. Wind becomes an aqueduct of dreams and wishes and screams and inhales and exhales. They dissipate into the air with a casual intensity that means the world. The Earth breathes, and that breath gives life. It also takes it away but does not destroy it.

I looked back down at the Place I Know Well and a sea of vibrant faces worshipping the sun, their future certain but in a way that seemed to allow full attention to right now.

When it was my turn to follow along in steady, blustery procession, I felt myself floating. Was I floating in spite of something or yielding to it? Were we always meant to float?

We joined hands and spiraled toward the clouds above where we landed, gently and sweetly bounding across the surface, the lightest and softest wool you could ever imagine. We fed the clouds and with our bodies we fell through and down, bursting into a million pieces, each one as whole as the next. We fed the sky, and we fed the soil. Trickling somewhere deep in the womb of the Earth, we felt her heartbeat and existed in synchronicity with it.

Who are you?

I am a lover. I love hard. I love so hard I don't know what to do with myself. I love so hard that sometimes I don't know how to feel it. I love so hard that I overflow. But remember what it means to overflow: it means to be so full yourself that you have the blessing of sharing.

When we finally awoke on the mountainside, we sat and watched it all over again. We met each other in big places, and we met each other in small places. And we met each other in places that felt exactly the right size.

You can see more than you think. What is the smallest thing you can possibly see? Where's the smallest place you can possibly go? Within the cone of Echinacea, you'll find on a mountaintop overlooking a valley, and the edge of an old forest is another forest, if you're small enough. This forest is different. The columns in this forest don't have leaves or branches. But they still provide a quiet resting place where you can hide from the sun and the sky and listen to the gentle breeze passing through like a quiet pipe organ. You lay with the wind and the small spider that finds shelter there, too.

There's something comforting about being small together. If you climbed to the top of one of these columns within the cone of Echinacea, would you find another forest that you didn't know existed?

Birch

A gate with no walls sits at the edge of a field. It's just a formality, an expression of gratitude and respect that need not be enforced. The birds of prey overhead beat their wings, sending gasps through the tall grass below. The bottomless horizon gently unfolds, offering glimpses of what hides behind it.

There's no need to walk, just swim. Let the current rippling through the grass carry you to the other side. You can sing back when the Earth sings to you.

In a field caressed by sunlight, in the shade of a Pine grove and neighboring mountains, is a path that leads to a forest that discovered how to trap the night under its canopy. When you move through the forest, don't be afraid to become the forest. Swing from the branches. Scurry across the ground. Smell the gentle citrus of the Pine. Let your feet touch the ground and reach upward until you can see the horizon and reach downward with your roots until they can join in kinship with the watering hole.

In the middle of the forest, sitting in quiet contemplation, is a solitary Birch. She sits with eyes closed, seeing all she is supposed to see. Our foreheads touch, infusing our understanding with that of each other's. We sat in quiet contemplation with eyes closed until the rains came and we watched her dissolve as her leaves rained down to meet the Earth once again.

When all has dissolved and the leaves have reunited with the ground, look out your window. Keep looking until it dissolves too.

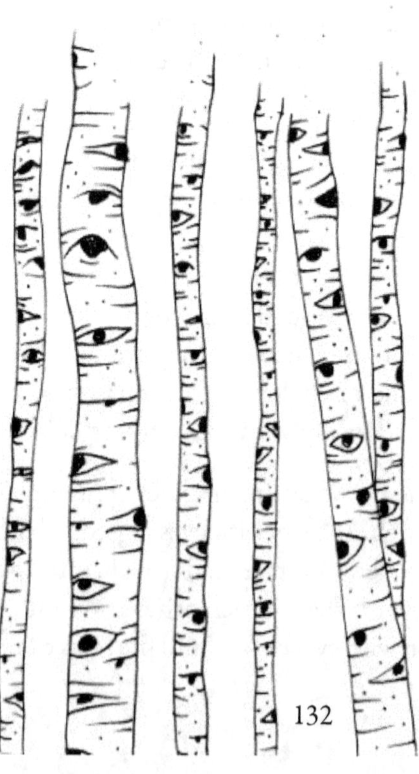

Elecampane

Deep in a womb you lay. Elecampane has prepared Earth's chrysalis for your slumber. The flowers above are singing. Their song vibrates each of your cells, each little piece of you that is hard at work becoming. Your lungs pulse with the vibration of the flowers. Your blood is like a small pond, each impact sending ripples that float through your core, undulating with each voice. Spirits dance through your veins.

We sing for ourselves. We sing for you. We sing for the bees and for the pure pleasure of feeling breath rush through our lungs toward the space that holds us. Even if just for a brief moment, we exist as a song suspended between ourselves and everything.

Elecampane says to find meaning in rest. Elecampane says to find sovereignty in surrender.

Your burial is not a death; death is a never-ending process. So is life. Your burial is where life finds restoration. In order for restoration to occur, something first must be given, creating the space for restoration to fill.

You give of yourself every day. You offer your life up to the world around you in exchange for the continual rush of life through you.

Let unshakeable trust in yourself invite vulnerability. Be vulnerable. Let others be vulnerable. Let others be vulnerable with whoever they want to be vulnerable with.

They call me Wild Sunflower because they know the sun is my home. Wherever it is, I find place. I know where my home is, and I can find it anywhere. I am always between the sunlight and the Earth; I am an edge walker between the terrestrial and the cosmic .

It was once said, *Enula campana reddit praecordia sana.*

Elecampane will the spirits sustain.

New England Aster

Stare down the barrel of a glittering, dazzling purple. It's like staring into the shoreline of a lake on a sunny summer day, a lake that is dancing to a choreography it dreams with the sun, birthing a purple sparkling disco ball.

How do you dream? Do you dream with the sun? When your photoreceptors are dulled by the absence of a partner, do they dream about the light? Do they remember what it feels like to connect with sunshine? During the day, does moonlight pull them into imagination?

"I am more than the sum of my parts, but I love each part dearly. I am an integrated being that my soul moves through. I become with each inhale and settle into becoming with each exhale."

My soul spreads from the tip of my roots to the tip of my shoots and seeps out into somewhere imaginable. My soul shakes hands with the sun and doesn't need to know her name. My soul shakes hands with the bacteria and the fungi and the small little world of life within the soil. My soul shakes hands with the Pearl Crescent caterpillar nuzzled against my leaves.

Remember who your soul shook hands with? Remember the gentle and comforting companion who aids in cycles of death and birth, carrying messages to their home? The one who finds comfort in vulnerability and home wherever the sun shines?

Remember the strong and subtle presence that softens hardened Earth, like you and me, with powerful murmurs? The one who is wholly self-assured?

Remember the mindful guide into one's inner sanctuary and the sanctuaries you didn't know surrounded you? The one who forges deep sweetness for those she loves?

Remember the one who is articulated by the infinite cycles of becoming and rest? The one who carries who she is with her and presents herself as an expression of forever unfolding?

Remember the one who tends to the world around her by spreading her seeds and noticing the becoming around her, and the becoming into her? The one who is a wise grandmother who helps us become who we are?

Remember the sweet one? Remember the one who embodies ritual and holds space for the sacred to manifest in authenticity and sincerity?

Remember the one who cares deeply about her home? Who introduces you to the magic of the mundane and the place I dwell and all of the life within it? A gentle soul that will introduce you to your neighbors, old and new, and teach you how to be one?

Remember the tender soul that brings out the tenderness in you? The one who holds space for the child you are and joins you in gratitude and wonder?

Remember the seer? She lets the wind of life flow through her and offers a hand to those who want to join? In the breath of life, she helps me find love, curiosity, rest, and kinship.

And in a circle in a field, we remember together. We sit, hand in hand in the sky, and we shout as we welcome the small flower blooming for the first time in that field in the sky.

Flowering Dogwood

Where is everything there is? Right here. Looking out at the world with a mind as empty and impressionable as the words on the page. Right here, in my delicate stamen making love to the wind. Right here, in a Black Bear's inhalation. Right here. Look no further, and you'll find everything there is.

Where is life found? Life is found where it is given space to reside. How do you hold life inside of you? How do you hold the world inside of you?

Flowering Dogwood holds life with gracious clarity. Behind her bark and within her wood is a strength that surpasses fluidity. You can be who you are while letting who you are flow through you. Millions of years of life in the making flow through our veins. It makes our heart beat. It holds our shakiest fears and strongest confidences. It propels each exhalation and cradles each inhalation. It floods you with love and the astute awareness of what creates your senses. It arrives, grounded in life without holding on to it.

Flowering Dogwood. Cornus florida. Petals of four. Bark that runs yellow. Roots that run red. Eternal exhalation. Gravity defined. Levity divine. Call me what you want, but you can only know me in the place that I am in.

We don't have to talk; we can just listen. Emptiness is full of wonder. It is full of possibility, like each empty word on this page woven into a meaning that is only as real as right now. In emptiness, find hereness. In my flowers, find a quatrain waiting to unfold, never to be heard again as anything more than the entrails of a spirit fragmented into someone's present.

Sassafras

You're soft, you know? You make me feel like my body is moving through jelly, slow enough to feel the way we embrace each other in a sticky sweetness. There's something beautiful about your spontaneity of form. When others look at you, they see the light greens and tender beiges of spring, followed by the fuzzy jade of summer, and the golden reds and yellows of fall. When I look at you, I see a kaleidoscope. When I close my eyes, I see it. I see the way you shine the sun and all of her colors back at me.

Sassafras has much to teach about mindful chewing. Take the tender leaf she offers you between your lips and feel her transform on your tongue. Feel her become medicine. Feel her become wonder and laughter.

When you tend to something, you do not leave it better than you left it, but you leave it different. You allow your presence to seep into harmony. You leave behind a stain, an impression, a harmony, that arose from the dissonance between the tension and transformation of that encounter. You press up against each other. And like a river flowing over stones or an ocean tumbling glass, you both leave changed.

You, too, are the world. When you soften your edges and experience a fractalization of self, you multiply your touchpoints. Feel more. Taste more. Touch more. Feel each particle of life as it flows over your skin, through your lungs, into your ears. Have you ever felt every particle of water that flowed through a river?

Sometimes I don't know where we're going. But the beautiful thing about not knowing is the opportunity to be. The opportunity to find out. The opportunity to hear a voice that you didn't know you could hear in a language that maybe you don't know. You don't have to know what's being said to find beauty in the voice. It might share something with you that lives far beyond words.

Think in color. Hear in visions of purple and emerald green. Feel music kiss your eardrums and see vibrations pulse through the air. It can be as simple as putting a fuzzy green leaf in your mouth and feeling it become something unexpected. Emptiness is a thick, thick feeling.

Serviceberry

I like where I landed. When I arrived here, I waited patiently. I waited until I could feel the wind and the rain and the soil. My roots explored their new home. They explored and experienced. They expanded and multiplied and became acquainted with that entire world underground, an infinity beyond one square foot of soil.

Once I realized where I was, I stretched my arms to the sky. I wiggled and reached. The sun awakened my eyes. The soil moistened my lips. I felt the heartbeat of a world once more and gave myself to it.

When I emerged into this new world, I settled into place. I met the sound of the Mockingbird and the rustle of the wind through my leaves. I met the rain and felt cool water drip down my stem. I was greeted by the sun, who awakens me every morning and reminds me when it's time to rest.

I like where I landed. The land orchestrates a symphony that is repeated and revised each year. We silently wait for our turn, emerging out of winter into the kindness of a spring day. We know when it's time to wake up. And as we wake up, we stretch and reach toward life and sunshine and deep down into the Earth from whence we came.

With each inhale. we become; with each exhale, we breathe ourselves back into the world. We are content in our world, not concerned with what lies beyond the place we're in. We know the world is okay without us, too.

Each plant takes their turn emerging, unfolding, and blooming, slowly and delicately, timed to place and attuned to being. We are always there, playing our part.

We deeply and sincerely know what it is to breathe.

Just like any good symphony, our symphony is held by lulls and swept away when the awareness and emergence of melodies and harmonies leap out to be caught. In slowness, we find contentedness. In taking our time, we find a perfect expression of who we are in the place that we're in, the place that created us, the place that makes us who we are.

And in return, we offer the irresistible sweetness of a berry; a small package that carries within it gratitude, hope, and giving. Through our offering, we're taken to new places and old places, where we'll find our bearings. When we realize we like the place we're in, we offer a life to that place; a life that bounds towards itself in a slow and steady procession that holds a whirlwind and meditation all in one.

Watch me and you'll see how much I like the place I'm in.

Hydrangea

Why wouldn't I be a plant to talk to? Why do you think we wouldn't have a chat? I greeted you first. I welcomed you into your new home while the rest of the yard was sleeping. Over-pruning and over-mulching meant an early end to summer. We weren't cared for as we should have been for a while now, and so before your arrival, the overgrowth of wildness in the yard was trimmed, to make space.

I think you were sad. Maybe we were, too. But the space that was made quickly filled and allowed those lying in wait to burst forth. Tending is a beautiful thing.

Hydrangea was there when I arrived. Her single blue bloom greeted us every morning, and on our return home from work. She let us know that someone was still here. That we'd all get a chance to meet after a cool winter's slumber. The life in that one blue bloom lived for all the yard for one later summer. A solo performance that is a prologue to the symphony to come.

Maybe things will go quiet again for a little while. Surely, they will. And in that silence, we'll miss each other, but we won't be gone. The groundhog will be hibernating in their den with the rabbits and the foxes and the snakes. We can still share and commune in rest.

But it isn't time yet. June has only just begun. Some of those who you met earlier this year will bed early. Some of those are ephemeral; not meant to last. They aren't gone; they're still there under the ground. Like the Bloodroot that seemed as if to disappear off the face of the Earth after only a short time. If you want to meet her now, you should go underground. She likes the darkness this time of year.

The Earth objectifies the flower, but only for a brief moment. The flower becomes externalized, finding its own internalization as an articulation of something greater than the sum of its parts.

I am not what you would call ephemeral. Something about her warmth sent shivers up my spine. When you feel a great void, she will fill it. Even an empty photo is a photo. Even an empty word is a word. Space is needed for worlds to appear.

The corymb of my flowers' heads is only possible through spacious coordination. No single flower takes up too much space. She knows where she is to land, to leave room for her sisters.

Maybe this is the end of the book. Maybe Hydrangea is here to lead us out and lead us on. The flowers don't tell the bees or the rain everything they know. Their teachings have seasons, too.

Hydrangea, my north star. Plant thinking reaches out, divides, and expands like tendrils. Over time, flowers emerge from the roots, the stems, and the branches and cluster into something touchable, smellable, admirable. This kind of thinking is not chaotic. It is an organized beauty that acknowledges connection where connection arises and thinks itself within relationship.

Plant thinking does not end at its bloom. The story continues, told in the honey of the bees and the chatter of the woodpecker. The cells that make up a bloom never forget who they once were.

We've been hibernating for a little while, in the ground, in the dark. The gentlest rain provides water for the flowers, seeping and absorbing slow enough to chat with their roots for a while.

We've been hibernating for a little while. But it's time to wake up, peek outside. *Don't forget to come up for air every now and then*, they say. So we arise. We introduce ourselves to the world.

As June draws to a start, we contemplate knowing together. We have shared pieces of our souls with each other, with ourselves, with the Earth and the Sky. But what is it to know? What is it that we walk away holding?

A circle closes but the center remains open. A Hydrangea blooms but the potential for blooming does not cease; it only persists, rests, and waits. I perceive the aliveness, intelligence, creativity, love of a plant through their signatures. These are crumbs and expressions left behind for me to hold and contemplate, to saturate my consciousness with a spacious emptiness. I will never know what it is like to be you, Hydrangea, but what I perceive is beautiful, pulsing, and alive. I am so grateful for your bloom, reminding me that life was not in wait, but living in restfulness in my yard before the return of spring.

I'm sure you've seen a Hydrangea somewhere; did you know she was so profound? Did you know how far she could take you? Don't concern yourself with the beating of your heart. Trust the millions of years of wisdom, living, breathing, and beating, to tell your heart what to do. We are a part of nature, a part of life, so we do not need to go further than ourselves to find it.

Look at the way we exist in the world. Our presence tells you something about who we are. Pay attention. Whispers come in so many shapes and forms.

This is not an end but a memoir of beginnings that will continue to bloom, wither, seed, and die. What a beautiful garden we have. Enjoy it today, because what is today if not eternity?

Epilogue

On a warm day in September in a small Austin apartment, I felt the voice of a plant for the first time. This plant was on the other side of Texas in the Chihuahuan Desert. This wasn't the first time a plant spoke to me, but it was the first time I listened. The conversation was brief, but in just a few short sentences, I was taught everything I needed to know about living.

"Would you like to experience death?" asked the Agave.

Life cannot be meaningless because life is meaning. To experience experience is to make sense, to be enlivened by the touch of the world, sometimes patiently guiding one through their scenic umwelt, other times capsizing the somatic boat before it has time to melt into the balancing act of the ocean of experience. My fingers create meaning when they touch a cold, subtly topographic stone surface. My eyes create meaning as they collide with the chromatic archway of a Rainbow. My nose creates meaning as it inhales the velvet entrails of a Lavender flower, a meaning that cannot be put into words but carries an entire life within it. Jeremy Lent says, "meaning is a function of connectedness, always participatory."

Meaning is a paradox. Meaning is all we have; a multiplicity of truths coexisting among the sea of lifeworlds that traverse it. And yet, meaning shatters upon contact. What is attempted to be channeled through language, art, movement, equations, and theories produces an incomplete picture, the completeness of which can never be captured. The only way to grasp meaning is to unclench your first.

"Death isn't extraordinary; we do it all the time," said the Agave.

And so I scream my soul to you alongside all of those whispering voices that co-create it. I will die a million times before I live a single day. And one day, like a potter recycling old clay, I will be softened and broken down, added to the collection of eager matter waiting to be formed into a new life. A new universe. And just like a seed awaiting germination, a language deep inside my bones stirred, one that calcified thousands of years ago.

With love,

Damiana	*Apple Mint*	*Echinacea*
Thistle	*Gingko*	*Birch*
Passionflower	*Hemp*	*Elecampane*
Sequoia	*Monarda*	*New*
Yellow Lotus	*Lemon Balm*	*England Aster*
Cedar	*Violet*	*Flowering*
Black Cohosh	*Rosemary*	*Dogwood*
Ghost Pipe	*Elderberry*	*Sassafras*
Chamomile	*Periwinkle*	*Serviceberry*
Tobacco	*Poison Ivy*	*Hydrangea*
Marigold	*Forsythia*	*Sydney*

Bibliography

Baluška, František and Stefano Mancuso. "Individuality, Self and Sociality of Vascular Plants." *Philosophical Transactions of the Royal Society B,* vol. 376, no. 1821, Feb. 2021.

Bonato, Bianca, et al. "Cracking the Code: A Comparative Approach to Plant Communication." *Communicative & Integrative Biology,* vol. 14, no. 1, Aug. 2021, pp. 167-185.

Buchmann, Stephen. *The Reason for Flowers: Their History, Culture, and Biology, and How They Change Our Lives.* Scribner, 2015.

Burd, Martin. "Colorful Language - It's How Aussie Birds and Flowers 'Speak.'" *The Conversation,* 25 Feb. 2014.

Chamovitz, Daniel. *What a Plant Knows: A Field Guide to the Senses.* Scientific American / Farrar, Straus and Giroux, 2017.

Donahue, Michelle Z. "Flowers Can Hear Buzzing Bees - and it Makes Their Nectar Sweeter." *National Geographic,* 15 January 2019.

Hall, Michael. *The Imagination of Plants: A Book of Botanical Mythology.* SUNY Press, 2019.

Holdrege, Craig. "The Wisdom of Plants - Craig Holdrege." *YouTube,* uploaded by The Nature Institute, 16 May 2024.

Gagliano, Monica, et al. "Tuned In: Plant Roots Use Sound to Locate Water." *Oecologia,* vol. 184, no. 1, May 2017, pp. 151-160.

Johnston, Lyla June. *Architects of abundance: Indigenous regenerative food and land management systems and the excavation of hidden history.* University of Alaska Fairbanks, PhD dissertation.

Jukes, Helen. *A Honeybee Heart Has Five Openings: A Year of Keeping Bees.* Pantheon Books, 2022.

Lent, Jeremy. *The Web of Meaning: Integrating Science and Traditional Wisdom to Find Our Place in the Universe.* New Society Publishers, 2021.

Marder, Michael. *Plant Thinking: A Philosophy on Vegetal Life.* Columbia University Press, 2013.

Sheldrake, Rupert. *The Science Delusion.* Coronet, 2020.

Veits, Marine, et al. "Flowers Respond to Pollinator Sound Within Minutes by Increasing Nectar Sugar Concentration." *Ecology Letters,* vol. 22, no. 9, Dec. 2018, pp. 1483-1492.

Villena, Julio, et al. "Receptors and Signaling Pathways for Recognition of Bacteria in Livestock and Crops: Prospects for Beneficial Microbes in Healthy Growth Strategies." *Fronties in Immuniology*, vol. 9, Sept. 2018.

Weber, Andreas. *The Biology of Wonder: Aliveness, Feeling and the Metamorphosis of Science.* Chelsea Green Publishing, 2016.

—. *Matter and Desire: An Erotic Ecology.* Chelsea Green Publishing, 2017.

Acknowledgements

I would like to begin by saying thank you to all my friends–the human and the more-than-human ones–who supported this vision in the ways they knew how. I'm grateful for all the plants that have been willing to spend time with me and share with me so the words on these pages could materialize. I'm also grateful for the little rental home in Asheville, North Carolina where this book was written. You likely won't be my home forever, but I'm glad you were able to hold the space for this writing and for all of the little moments that make up this book.

Thank you to my editor, Will Brown, for helping to clean up the edges and for helping me make sense of what we are trying to say. Thank you to Peter Webb, the author of the Foreword and a dear friend, for cheering the stories on as they've unraveled and for encouraging me to stay mindful and curious. Your friendship, which first budded with this book and I hope lasts a long time, means a lot to me. Thank you to Heather Sanderson for your guidance in all things plant relationship, writing, and publishing.

I'm grateful for my family and friends for offering the space and encouragement to write this book. I'm also grateful to my partner for being a wonderful listener as I've rambled on about my ideas, philosophies, successes, and failures. This book wouldn't have been possible without all of the relationships that sustain me.

About the Author

Sydney Kale is a phenomenologist, ecologist, and plant-lover. She is currently a Ph.D. student of Wisdom Studies at Ubiquity University, with an academic focus on plant intelligence and phenomenology. She holds an M.S. in Environmental Studies and Sustainability from Unity College and an M.A. in Movement, Mind, and Ecology from Schumacher College. During the latter, she wrote her dissertation, "For the Love of Plants. An Inquiry into Science, Subjectivity, and a Decoupling of Human and Being," with Damiana. Her academic studies and creative writing explore what it is to be plant and what it is to be human from the perspectives of ecology, kinship, and entanglement. For more information, visit www.sydneykale.com.